Pointed
and
Personal

Ray Markham

Pointed
and
Personal

Ray Markham

Contents

Dedication

*To my wife Sheila, and my mother Dora,
in appreciation of their unfailing love,
support and prayers.*

All Bible quotations are from the
New International Version unless otherwise stated.

Abbreviations:
GNB – Good News Bible
KJV – King James Version (Authorised version)
LB – Living Bible
NIV – New International Version
TEV – Today's English Version

ISBN 1-903921-04-X

Published by
AUTUMN HOUSE
Alma Park, Grantham, Lincs, England, NG31 9SL

2 4 6 8 10 9 7 5 3 1

Introduction

No matter how many times I read the parables of Jesus, they always speak to me in both a pointed and a personal way.

They point out my personal shortcomings, encouraging me to change my ways and to evaluate my attitudes. They are like pointed arrows, which penetrate my personal defences and unfailingly hit their intended target.

Some remind me of God's boundless love, mercy and grace towards me personally. Others pointedly remind me what God expects of me.

As you read this book, may these wonderful parables of Jesus speak to you, too, in a pointed and a personal way: challenging you, yet encouraging you, as they do me.

Ray Markham

The aims of this book

It is of the greatest importance that all those of us who count ourselves members of God's Kingdom actually know and understand what Jesus taught, and how to put His teachings into practice in our daily lives.

In this book, I have attempted to provide a thorough and thought-provoking analysis of the teaching of Jesus contained in the parables. I have endeavoured to write in an imaginative style that is easy to read and understand. When writing, I had two particular aims in mind. Firstly, to explain what Jesus taught clearly, concisely and cogently. Secondly, to apply these teachings in practical ways to everyday life.

This book provides the basic points to be drawn from Jesus' teaching, for the benefit of Christians who are young in the faith, and also a great deal of material for the more mature Christian to reflect on, including many references for further study.

I also had in mind group leaders who were looking for a book which would help them prepare studies on the teachings of Jesus, or guide a group through them. That is why, at the end of each chapter, there is a carefully prepared set of questions designed to promote discussion about, and encourage application of, the teaching in that section. The group leader can either select from the comprehensive list provided, or use them all over a number of sessions. The questions can also be used to aid personal study and reflection.

If readers find that this book helps them to understand the teachings of Jesus contained in the parables, while at the same time enabling them to see how they can be put into practice, I shall be delighted to have succeeded in what I set out to do.

All Bible quotations are from the New International Version unless otherwise stated.

An introduction to the parables

Definition

The word 'parable' comes from the Greek word *parabole*, which means 'a placing beside'. It is a form of illustration which compares something unfamiliar to something familiar so we can understand it. By placing the two alongside, the teller of the parable helps us to see the meaning of the unfamiliar by linking it closely to a situation with which we are already familiar.

In His parables, Jesus used everyday objects, relationships and situations to help the people then, and us now, to understand deep spiritual truths. They were familiar with farming, weddings, journeys, clothing, vineyards, family life, buildings, sheep, jewellery, seeds, burglary, money, friends, parties, and people from all walks of life. So these made up the material He drew on for His parables.

Parables in the Old Testament

However, Jesus did not invent the parable. It was a type of illustration with which the Jews were already acquainted, although no one has used this particular method with such power, variety and effectiveness as Jesus did, or with such frequency.

✳ Stories

The parables we find in the Old Testament fall into three categories. Firstly, there are the parables which bring teaching through means of a story. Jotham tells the people of Shechem the parable of the trees (Judges 9:8-15). Perhaps a more well-known example is the parable of the lamb, told by the prophet

Nathan to King David (2 Samuel 12:1-6). Another prophet, Ezekiel, used parables on four occasions to bring God's teaching to the people (Ezekiel 17; 19:1-9; 23; 24:3-5). The vast majority of Jesus' parables fall into this category.

✳ Prophecies

Secondly, there are the prophetic parables, which speak about events affecting the nation of Israel. The Psalmist uses the picture of a vine brought out of Egypt, planted, prospering, fruitful, yet now in a bad way. He pleads with God for the restoration and salvation of the nation, and speaks of a figure he calls 'the son of man' (Psalm 80:8-17). The prophet Isaiah tells of a vineyard being planted, which yielded only bad fruit (Isaiah 5:1-7).

The symbol of the vine and the vineyard as representing the Jewish nation occurs several times in the Old Testament. Jesus Himself uses it most notably in the Parable of the Tenants [see chapter 4]. He deliberately links His parable to that of Isaiah by including a watchtower and a winepress in His description of the vineyard, and goes on to prophesy what will happen to Him at the hands of the Jews, and the severe consequences of this.

✳ Actions

Thirdly, there are the acted parables. These are where points are made through actions or activities being undertaken. The prophet Ahijah tore a garment into twelve pieces in front of Jeroboam, who was to become King of Israel (1 Kings

11:29-32). A prophet of God acted as a prisoner of war to make a point to King Ahab (1 Kings 20:35-43). God caused a vine to grow over Jonah to provide him with shade, a vine which was then eaten away the next day, allowing God to make His point to the prophet (Jonah 4:5-11).

But perhaps it is the prophet Jeremiah who is most noted for the use of acted parables. Being obedient to God, he made an ox yoke and wore it day after day to make the point that the king of Babylon would put a yoke of captivity upon the Jews (Jeremiah 27, 28). On a previous occasion, God had told him to buy a linen belt, bury it, and leave it there until it was ruined and completely useless. This was to show the people that God would ruin their great pride (chapter 13). Probably the most famous example was when he bought a field at Anathoth. It was quite clear by this time that the Babylonian army was going to conquer the land and occupy it, so there was no chance he would ever use it. But it was a statement of faith in God that one day the Jews would return, and his descendants would farm the land (chapter 32).

The most notable acted parable in the ministry of Jesus is when He washes and dries the feet of His disciples, which is then followed by teaching about their serving one another (John 13:1-17). It could be said that the withering of the fig tree is also an acted parable, bringing a warning of God's judgement on Israel (Mark 11:13, 14, 20-22).

Why did Jesus speak in parables?

The disciples asked Jesus this very question (Matthew 13:10). In reply, the reason He gave was twofold. He did it to reveal, and at the same time to conceal (13:11-17). He used parables to reveal spiritual truth to those who were sincerely seeking. Because such people were receptive to the truth, and were keen to discover it, they would understand what Jesus was teaching. On the other hand, these same parables would conceal spiritual truth from those who were too lazy to discover it, or were too stubborn to see it; all they would hear would be stories without any apparent meaning, which is why Jesus consistently said: '"He who has ears, let him hear"' (13:9).

Another reason why Jesus spoke in parables was to get His listeners to work out for themselves what He was teaching. The parable of 'The Good Samaritan' provides us with an excellent example of this. Instead of simply answering the question He is asked, Jesus tells this story. At the end of it, He turns to the questioner, and asks him a question. This is to make the man answer his original question for himself. Jesus isn't usually as direct as this, but His aim is always to make us work out the spiritual truth the parables are teaching. Rarely does He actually spell out the meaning for us. It is obvious for those who have ears to hear. Jesus knows that we are far more likely to retain what we have been taught if we have to work it out for ourselves, rather than just being told.

As Matthew points out, the fact that Jesus used parables was actually a fulfilment of prophecy: '"I will open my mouth in parables, I will utter things hidden since the creation of the world"' (13:35).

Chapter 1

SHORT SHARP SHOCKS

The Kingdom of God

Jesus described the spiritual truth He was revealing by means of His parables as ' "The knowledge of the secrets of the kingdom of heaven" ' (Matthew 13:11). The Kingdom of God was the central theme of His preaching and teaching. According to Mark, He began His ministry with these words: ' "The time has come . . . the Kingdom of God is near" ' (Mark 1:15a).

So what did this phrase 'The Kingdom of God' mean already to the people who heard Jesus? The Jews regarded God exclusively as their King. This went back to the time of Moses, when what we call the Old Covenant [Testament] had been established at Mount Sinai. Ever since then, there had existed a special relationship between them and God: they were His 'chosen people'. As far as the Jews were concerned, God's Kingdom was the Jewish nation; they alone acknowledged His sovereignty. Unlike the other rulers around, their kings did not claim absolute power. The Jewish nation was a theocracy. It was ruled by God, and the kings were answerable to Him.

✳ Ideas take shape

For the 800 years or so prior to the coming of Jesus, the Jews had experienced nothing but occupation or exile. First it was the Assyrians, then the Babylonians, then the Persians, then the Greeks, and now it was the Romans. Ideas about the Kingdom of God started to take shape during the period of the Babylonian exile, which began in 586BC. The prophecies of that time found in the books of Ezekiel and Isaiah 40-55 contrast the peoples' sufferings then with a better time to come. This inspired them to keep on hoping for the coming of God's Kingdom through all the bad times they were experiencing. During the time leading up to the coming of Jesus, there was great anticipation that God was going to help them soon: the Kingdom of God was on its way!

They believed that God would send the Messiah to deliver them, though they had different ideas about Him. They also had different ideas about what the Kingdom of God would be like. God was going to be in charge, but what would this actually mean? For a group called the Zealots it meant that the Jews would govern their own country according to God's laws after the Romans had been thrown out by force. As far as the Essenes were concerned, the Kingdom of God would begin with a kind of heavenly war against all evil powers and all evil people. The upshot? Everything wrong would be destroyed, and the resulting Paradise would be the Kingdom of God. In whatever way they thought it would be brought about, the Jews believed that it would be an everlasting Kingdom, for them alone.

✳ Jesus and the Kingdom

When Jesus uses this phrase, He talks about it in two ways: the Kingdom of God is actually present among us now; yet we shall not see it in all its fullness until some time in the future. It has arrived with Him, and its presence is being shown in the work He is doing. His acts of healing and exorcism bear witness to the fact that He is reclaiming the world for its rightful King, from the evil one who holds it in his grip.

It is not a kingdom made up of territory that can be marked on a map: it is a kingdom made up of people from all nations who accept God's rule in their hearts, and have given their lives to Him and to His service. And, unlike the situation in the kingdoms of the world, its members are not separated from their enemies, but live cheek by jowl with them.

The Kingdom of God is about a new society that has different standards and values from the kingdoms of the world, and these are to be seen in the lifestyles of those who belong to it. Their relationship with God is not for this life only: it will continue into eternity, when the Kingdom will be known in all its fullness. Jesus indicated that, at a particular point in time, He would return in power and glory to judge the world and bring in the Kingdom of God in all its completeness and perfection. His resurrection opened the way for that future fulfilment.

Several of Jesus' parables are about the Kingdom of God. Although He never precisely defined this phrase, many clues as to what it is like are contained within these parables. They vary in length, and are often introduced with the words, 'The kingdom of heaven is like', used thirty-two times in Matthew, or 'The kingdom of God is like', as found in Mark and Luke. Part of the brilliance of these parables is that many of them contain two layers of meaning: one which was particularly appropriate for when Jesus told it; the other one speaking into the life and times of the first Christians, much of which applies to us. Bearing in mind their beliefs, we believe these parables must have come like a series of short sharp shocks to His Jewish listeners.

The Parable of the Weeds
Matthew 13:24-30, 36-43

In this parable, Jesus says that the Kingdom is like a man sowing good seed in his field. Eventually it becomes apparent that there are weeds in the field, growing side by side with the wheat. These weeds were probably darnel, which looks very much like wheat at first, but can be clearly distinguished after a while. The servants ask the owner where the weeds have come from, since he sowed only wheat. He explains that an enemy has been at work. They then ask if he wants them to root out the weeds. The owner says that to do this may mean pulling up some of the wheat as well, so they are to wait until harvest time when both can be removed together and sorted out. The weeds can then be burnt, and the wheat gathered into His barn.

The meaning of the parable is made clear in verses 36-43. The field is a picture of the world, with believers and non-believers living side by side. The growing of the wheat and the weeds together refers to the time-span between the life of Jesus and His Second Coming. When Jesus, the Son of Man, returns, He will bring the age in which we are living to an end; the harvest will take place, and God's judgement will be meted out.

Inclusive, not exclusive
The shock for the Jews was that God's Kingdom was not

exclusive to them, but involved the whole world. While they were quite convinced that Gentiles would certainly come under the judgement of God, they were not so content with the idea that judgement was coming their way too.

Jesus has already broached this subject with them before (Matthew 8:11, 12), telling them that in heaven there will be those '"from the east and the west"', in other words, Gentiles, sitting down at the feast '"with Abraham, Isaac and Jacob"', the father figures of the Jewish nation, known as the Patriarchs, each of whom showed great faith in God. '"The subjects of the kingdom"' represent the Jews who do not show faith in Jesus, the Son of God, and will therefore be excluded from His Kingdom. They are not going to be there as of right, just because they are Jews, as they have always assumed. They are going to be in God's Kingdom in heaven only if they, too, repent and put their faith and trust in Jesus.

Inescapable

Many people today are shocked by the idea of each one of us having to face God's judgement. Unpalatable though the concept may be to some, it is clearly there in the teaching of Jesus: for example, in Matthew 5:21, 22; 12:36; 22:13. It is inescapable. The writer to the Hebrews puts it quite bluntly: 'Just as man is destined to die once, and after that to face judgement, so Christ was sacrificed once to take away the sins of many people; and he will appear a second time, not to bear sin, but to bring salvation to those who are waiting for him' (Hebrews 9:27, 28).

We have no need to fear God's judgement if we have responded to Jesus' sacrifice on the cross and asked His for-giveness for our sins. Jesus paid the price so that we don't have to. And when He comes again, this time in all His power and glory, the Kingdom will be revealed in all its fullness.

The Parable of the Growing Seed

Mark 4:26-29

In this parable, the seed is scattered on the ground, and grows without any further help from the sower. In fact, he doesn't have the slightest idea as to how the growth is effected (27, 28). It is not brought about by his skill or intervention: the process is outside his control. There is also an inevitability about it: he can't stop the growth, even if he wants to.

The meaning of this parable is that we must be faithful in sowing the Gospel of the Kingdom, but it is by the Spirit of God that the seed bears fruit in peoples' lives and causes the Kingdom to grow. The harvest may refer to the results that we see now as people are brought into the Kingdom, or it may look forward to the time when Jesus will come again and harvest the results of His work.

The growth of the Kingdom is inevitable. Nothing, not even all the works of the enemy, can stop it, because it is a supernatural process that God will one day bring to glorious fruition.

The Parable of the Mustard Seed

Matthew 13:31, 32
(Mark 4:30-32; Luke 13:18, 19)

This parable is also about growth: how the Kingdom is growing rapidly. The mustard seed was the smallest of all the seeds used by farmers. 'Small as a grain of mustard seed' was a frequently used Jewish saying. Yet in spite of its small beginnings, in a short time it could grow into a very large plant, even as high as two metres.

Jesus is saying that the Kingdom has come, and is growing quickly. It is already casting its shadow for those who want to shelter under its branches and make it their dwelling-place. He predicts that it will continue to show remarkable growth, even in a hostile environment which wants to see it destroyed. From its small beginnings in Palestine, it would spread rapidly throughout the world. The first Christians were seeing that being fulfilled in their lifetimes through the missionary work of the apostles.

Once again, His Jewish listeners would have been shocked by the idea that the Kingdom is a place which is open to all peoples. The word 'birds' was often used to refer to foreigners, meaning Gentiles, as in Daniel 4:12. Everyone is included in the invitation to the Kingdom of Heaven.

The Parable of the Yeast

Matthew 13:33

This is a parable about transforming power. Yeast could either be used as a symbol of a good influence, as in this case, or a bad one, as in Mark 8:15, where Jesus warns the disciples to '"Watch out for the yeast of the Pharisees and that of Herod"'.

The flour represents the whole world, which would be transformed by the yeast of Jesus' teaching as it spread abroad in the power and under the direction of the Holy Spirit. And that work is ongoing until Jesus comes again.

The Parable of the Hidden Treasure and the Pearl
Matthew 13:44-46

Both these parables mean that it is worthwhile giving up everything to become a member of the Kingdom. Once again, the Jews would have been shocked to discover that they had to do something to become members of the Kingdom: they were not automatically a part of it.

The man who accidentally came across the hidden treasure was prepared to buy the whole field in order to possess it. Similarly, some people stumble across the Gospel of Jesus when it is probably the furthest thing from their minds. For example, there are many testimonies from people who have found Bibles placed by the Gideons in hotel rooms or hospital wards, and been spoken to by the Spirit of God while reading it, and have become members of God's Kingdom as a result.

Others, like the merchant who discovered the pearl of great value, might have been actively seeking God for some time, and eventually have found Him in Jesus. Nothing in our lives is of greater worth than knowing Jesus and being members of His Kingdom.

The Parable of the Banquet
Matthew 22:1-10; Luke 14:15-24

There are many similarities between the accounts of the banquet parable in the two gospels: a fact which convinces some commentators that they are actually variations of the same story. However, there are some interesting differences, which we will note as we go along.

Come

In both cases, a banquet is prepared, and the guests are invited. The parable reflects the custom of the day, which was to issue two invitations. The first announced the event; the second informed the invited guests that everything was ready.

Whereas in Luke's account it is 'A certain man' (16) who is the host, in Matthew's it is 'a king' (2). And more than that, the King is preparing it 'for his son' (2). Matthew, who wrote his gospel with Jewish readers in mind, wants to make it absolutely clear to them that this is a parable about the coming of the Messiah, who is also the Son of God.

A banquet was already a well-known symbol among the Jews for the Kingdom of the Messiah. This Kingdom has now arrived with Jesus, and demands a response. The servants are sent out to tell the invited guests, who represent the Jews, that it is now time to come to the banquet, because everything is ready (Matthew 22:3, 4; Luke 14:17).

Excuses, excuses, excuses

In Matthew's account, the invited guests simply pay no attention and go off, 'one to his field, another to his business' (5). In Luke's account, this is developed further, as they give their excuses for not responding to the invitation (18-20). The 'field' stands for possessions; the 'oxen' are a symbol of work, money and career; 'just got married' represents family commitments.

These are the three areas that tend to dominate our lives today. For the invited guests, these were more important than their relationship with God and being part of His Kingdom. This is not to say that there is anything wrong with giving them a high priority in our lives. But it is important that we prayerfully consider whether they have in fact taken the place of what should be the highest priority in our lives. It's so easy for them to become excuses for not serving God in the way that He requires.

I heard of a church in the USA where the pastor got so fed up with members of his congregation making excuses for not attending Sunday services that he made the following announcement: 'To make it possible for everyone to attend church next Sunday, we are going to have a special "No Excuse Sunday". Cots will be placed in the foyer for those who say, "Sunday is my only day to sleep in." Murine will be available for those with tired eyes – from watching television too late on Saturday night. We will have steel helmets for those who say, "The roof would cave in if I ever came to church." Blankets will be provided for those who think the church is too cold, and fans for those who think the church is too hot. We will have hearing aids for those who say, "The pastor speaks too softly," and cotton wool for those who say he preaches too loudly. Score cards will be available for those who wish to list the hypocrites present. Some relatives will be in attendance for those who like to go visiting on Sunday. There will be 100 TV dinners for those who cannot go to church and cook dinner also. One section will be devoted to trees and grass for those who like to seek God in nature. Finally, the sanctuary will be decorated with both Christmas poinsettias and Easter lilies for those who have never seen the church without them.'

The Kingdom extended

Their refusal to respond to his message so enrages the King that he has them destroyed and their city burned (7). Some see in this a prediction of the events which occurred in the year AD70 when the Roman armies razed the city of Jerusalem to the ground, leaving only one wall of the platform on which the Temple was built standing. This became known as 'The Wailing Wall'. For others, it is a picture of the severity with which God regarded the Jews' lack of response, and the subsequent broadening of the invitation to include 'anyone you find' (9).

There are two stages to this as set out in Luke's account. Initially, the servants are to bring in 'the poor, the crippled, the blind and the lame' (21), representing the outcasts and sinners of Jewish society. The servants are then told to 'Go out to the roads and country lanes and make them come in' (23), representing those who were outside the Jewish community, namely, the Gentiles. This detail would have been of great significance to such people, showing as it did that they were welcome in God's Kingdom, which was no longer exclusively for the Jews. For Luke, it is vital that his fellow Gentiles should understand this point, so he emphasises it throughout his gospel.

Groups of Jews, like the Pharisees, who regarded themselves as righteous in God's sight because they strove to fulfil all the requirements of the Law of Moses, would have been shocked and offended by this parable. First of all, they were being told that unless they responded to the teaching of Jesus and accepted Him as the Son of God and the Messiah, they had no place in the Kingdom of God. Matthew emphasises this by continuing his account of this parable to include the moment when the King – with drastic results – finds someone present at the banquet who is not wearing wedding clothes (11-14). The point he is probably making is that this particular individual thought he could gain entry to the kingdom by being clothed in his own righteous acts; in other words, through his own efforts in obeying all the laws of Moses. However, the only acceptable clothing is that given by the King himself, which Jesus has come to bring. The prophet Isaiah describes it as a 'garment of salvation' and a 'robe of righteousness' (Isaiah 61:10). Interestingly, the same prophet describes our own righteous acts as 'filthy rags' (64:6). Perhaps that's what the intruder was wearing, although he might not have realised it. No one can enter the Kingdom of God by virtue of any good deeds he may have done.

Secondly, they were being told that the outcasts and sinners of Jewish society could gain entry to the Kingdom, a notion which was as unthinkable as it was unacceptable. And thirdly, if that wasn't enough to contend with, that God's Kingdom was being extended to include the despised Gentile nations and peoples. Hearing parables like these would have stiffened their resolve to be rid of this teacher from Nazareth at the earliest possible opportunity.

A place for everyone

Apparently, a German hotelier who lived near Cologne wanted to raise money for charity, so he prepared a table some 2,606 feet long. An estimated 20,000 guests came to the party and lined up for a long, sumptuous meal at what its promoter billed as the longest buffet table ever set. The banqueting table that God has prepared is open to all people of the world, and is large enough to accommodate all those who respond to His invitation.

Questions for group study

SHORT SHARP SHOCKS

The Kingdom of God
Background
1 What did the phrase 'The Kingdom of God' mean to the Jews at the time of Jesus?

Discuss
2 How did the Zealots' view of this Kingdom differ from that of the Essenes?
3 What two aspects of the Kingdom do we find in Jesus' teaching?
4 In what respects is the Kingdom of God different from the kingdoms of the world?
5 When will this Kingdom be known in all its fullness?

The Parable of the Weeds
Review
6 What do the field, the wheat, the weeds and the harvest each represent?
7 What is the meaning of this parable?

Discuss
8 What would the Jews have found shocking about this parable?

9 What other picture had Jesus previously used which would have challenged their understanding of the Kingdom?

10 Why are people today shocked by the idea of each one of us having to face God's judgement?

Apply
11 How are we as Christians to view God's judgement?

The Parable of the Growing Seed
Review
12 What do the seed and thc harvest each represent?

Discuss
13 What caused the seed to grow?

Apply
14 What implications does this have for us as we sow the Gospel in people's lives?

15 What encouragement can we take from the fact that the growth of the Kingdom is inevitable?

The Parable of the Mustard Seed
Review
16 What does this parable teach about the Kingdom?

Discuss

17 Why did Jesus use the mustard seed in particular to illustrate His point?

18 What is the significance of the phrase 'the birds of the air'?

19 What was Jesus teaching here that would have shocked His Jewish listeners?

Apply

20 What encouragement is there for us in this?

The Parable of the Yeast
Review

21 What do the flour and the yeast each represent?

22 What is the meaning of this parable?

Apply

23 What part do we have to play in this?

The Parable of the Hidden Treasure and the Pearl
Review

24 What do the treasure and the pearl both represent?

25 What do both these parables mean?

Discuss

26 Why would the Jews have been shocked by this teaching?

27 What differences are there in the ways the people in the parable discover their find?

Apply

28 What can we learn from this as we seek to bring the Gospel to people?

The Parable of the Banquet

Background

29 Why was it the custom to issue two invitations to a banquet?

30 For what was a banquet already a well-known symbol among the Jews?

Discuss

31 For Matthew, what is the significance of the fact that Jesus talks about a king who is preparing the banquet for his son?

32 What is the significance of the fact that it is now time for the guests to come to the banquet?

Review

33 How did the invited guests respond to the invitation to come now?

Discuss

34 What do the three excuses represent?

Apply

35 How does this serve as a warning for us?

Discuss

36 What different interpretations have been given to the king's angry reaction to his guests' lack of response?

Review

37 What are the two stages of response as set out in Luke's account?

Discuss

38 Who are represented by these two groups?

39 What was the significance of the second stage for Luke?

40 Why would the Pharisees in particular have been shocked and offended by this parable?

41 What point does the discovery of and dealings with the man not wearing wedding clothes make?

Apply

42 What can we learn from this about entry into the Kingdom?

For personal prayer and reflection

Do I rejoice that I have no need to fear God's judgement?

Do I back up my witnessing with the prayer that the Holy Spirit will water the seed and bring it to fruition?

Do I need to broaden my vision to see how God's Kingdom is growing throughout the world?

Am I always on the look-out for people with whom I can share my faith?

Have possessions, work, money or family commitments assumed a higher priority than God in my life?

Am I wearing a 'robe of righteousness', or am I relying on my own 'filthy rags' to get me into God's Kingdom?

Chapter **2**

ROOT AND FRUIT

The Parable of the Sower

Matthew 13:3-9, 18-23
(also Mark 4:1-20; Luke 8:4-15)

Introduction

Although this parable is not actually introduced by the words 'The kingdom of heaven is like', it is clearly a story about the Kingdom, showing the various responses of people to it. Matthew certainly thinks that, placing it as he does at the beginning of his collection of Kingdom parables.

The Sower, the Seed and the Soil

This is a parable about a sower who sows his seed in the field. The seed falls into different types of soil, with consequent results. The correct term for this kind of sowing is 'broadcasting'. The sower would walk up and down the field with a large basket hanging from his neck, throwing handfuls of seed from it to the left and to the right as he progressed.

This was a common sight in Jesus' time. Unlike today, when seed drills place the seed exactly where the farmer wants it to be, the broadcast seed would land wherever. It is from this process that the BBC took its name: an appropriate one, considering they broadcast their programmes to wherever, and get a range of responses as a result.

There are three layers of meaning to this parable. In each case, the sower represents the bringer of the message; the seed is the message itself; the four types of soil or ground stand for typical reactions and responses from people to the message.

First of all, the sower represents Jesus; the seed He sows is the message of the Kingdom; the soil stands for the Jews who heard Him. Secondly, the sower represents all those who seek to bring people to accept Jesus as their Saviour; the seed is the Gospel message; the soil stands for those who are not yet Christians. Thirdly, the sower represents the Holy Spirit and those whom He uses to teach the word of God; the seed is the teaching of Jesus and that of the Bible as a whole; the soil stands for all Christians. It would be a mistake to think that this parable is just about what happens when the Gospel is preached. There is far more to it than that. The challenge of this parable is: Which type of ground best describes me?

Hard ground (Matthew 13:4, 19)

Some seed fell along the path that ran by the side of the field, and in some cases even went across it. It was soon gobbled up by the birds, something that Jesus' listeners would have seen happen many times.

There were those who heard what Jesus said, but refused to allow His message to take root in their hearts and minds. They were not even prepared to try to understand what He was saying and the implications of it for them. Their preconceptions of the Kingdom were being challenged, and they didn't want to know. They did not allow the message to have any impact on their lives, so it bore no fruit for the Kingdom, and they remained outside of it.

Similarly, whenever we communicate the Gospel, there will be people who refuse to allow the message to take root in their hearts and minds, no matter how many times they hear it. They will not even try to understand it, let alone accept its implications; so it will have little impact on them and bear no fruit. Added to which, Satan has no intention of letting them contemplate what they have heard, and will use any means possible to remove what has been sown. Some people also have strong preconceptions about God, the universe and all that, and don't take kindly to having their ideas challenged. This can all be very discouraging, but instead of allowing ourselves to be dragged down by it, let's use it as a stimulus to pray even more fervently that God's Holy Spirit will water that hard ground so that it will become receptive to the Gospel.

Let's also remember that Jesus Himself experienced discouragement during His ministry (John 6:66), and that some didn't even believe when He appeared to them risen from the dead (Matthew 28:17b). Jesus warned his followers to expect rejection (Luke 10:16), insults and even persecution; all of which should be a cause for rejoicing (Matthew 5:11, 12).

It is also possible to be a Christian, even of many years' standing, and yet be this type of ground. This happens when we do not allow the teachings we have heard, or what the Holy

Spirit has shown us during our personal devotions, to take root in our hearts and minds and change us, making us more like Christ. This is often because we don't like what we're hearing, so we harden our hearts and minds to what God wants to plant in our lives. The result is that we make little progress in our Christian walk, and find ourselves no further on with God now than we were years ago.

To put it simply: if there's no root, there'll be no fruit. We have an enemy who is only too well aware of this, and is constantly seeking to snatch away that which God has sown in us before it can take root and grow. Satan will rob us of the Word of God spoken into our lives if we don't keep hold of it and put his 'birds' to flight. He doesn't want us to meditate on God's word, to take time to understand it, to allow it to penetrate and have an impact on our lives. He wants us to become ground that is hardened to the Word of God and consequently bears no fruit.

The path was such hard ground mainly because it did not have the benefit of being ploughed. Perhaps, in the words of the prophet Hosea, we need to 'break up' our 'unploughed ground' with God's help, and 'seek the Lord', so that we may become receptive once more (Hosea 10:12).

Rocky ground (Matthew 13:5, 6, 20, 21)

Some seed fell on ground where there were rocks and not much depth of soil. It sprang up quickly, but when the sun shone the plants were scorched and withered away, because they had little or no root.

There were those who heard what Jesus said, and responded to His message enthusiastically. However, when they experienced opposition, and began to realise fully what was involved in being disciples, they fell away. Their commitment, like the soil, was 'shallow' and lacked depth. We have already seen how many of Jesus' disciples left Him when they realised the implications of being members of the Kingdom (John 6:66).

Similarly, there are sometimes people who respond to the Gospel message with an initial burst of enthusiasm, but often, unfortunately, it doesn't last. When the heat is on, in the form of trials, problems, difficulties, rejection, ostracism, even persecution, they wither away. Their commitment was nothing more than bubble and froth, which burst under the pressure and was blown away.

Things were certainly 'hot', to say the least, at the time when this parable was being recorded by the gospel writers. By then, persecution had become a fact of life for many Christians in the Roman Empire, which makes this section of the parable particularly poignant. Some did fall away from their faith in those brutal times, but the vast majority were prepared to suffer martyrdom by being set alight as torches, by being thrown to the lions as part of the afternoon's entertainment in the amphitheatre, or by any number of awful deaths that the Romans dreamt up in their bid to stamp out this new religion of Christianity. People were amazed when they saw the courage of these martyrs and the depth of their commitment to what they believed, with the result that Christianity grew rapidly and spread throughout the Empire, rather than being eliminated.

The tree withstands the storm because it has put down deep roots. If we are to withstand the pressures that we experience as Christians, and stand firm in the face of the storms which will assuredly come our way, then we need to be well rooted and grounded in the Word of God, and have a deep relationship with our Father.

The roots of the tree grow deeper day by day. They can't

suddenly be driven deep into the ground when the storm begins. In the same way, we need to deepen our knowledge of God's Word and our personal relationship with Him on a daily basis, so that when the sun comes up and things start to get 'hot', we do not wither and die, but draw strength from Him and His Word to see us through.

Thorny ground
(Matthew 13:7, 22; Mark 4:7, 19; Luke 8:7, 14)

Other seed fell on ground where thorn bushes had also taken root. Apparently, these sprang up later and choked the seed which had put down roots and was growing so nicely and impressively. Luke's account says that the thorn bushes actually 'grew up with it and choked the plants'. The more the plants progressed, and the more fruitful they showed signs of becoming, the more the thorn bushes asserted themselves and the more they swamped the plants.

It is a sure thing that as soon as people allow God's word to take root, and start to show any signs of bearing fruit, Satan will try to choke them. Jesus experienced this in His ministry: it is clearly reflected in the Parable of the Banquet (see chapter 1). Similarly, there are many instances of people gladly accepting the message of the Gospel, making an excellent start in their Christian lives, but then fading away or not making the progress they should.

But this type of ground does not just represent people at the time of Jesus, or new converts: it can apply to anyone who allows his commitment to God to be compromised in any way. And it can happen so easily, because Satan is very subtle, often using perfectly justifiable things to choke us.

Four particular areas we need to watch out for are identified in the various accounts. These are: 'the worries of this life', 'wealth' and 'riches', 'pleasures', and 'the desires for other things'. The subtlety of the thorny ground is twofold. Firstly, none of these areas is wrong in itself. It is not wrong to be concerned about our families, our jobs and our relationships; nor is it wrong to earn money, to enjoy the pleasures of life, or to have possessions. What is wrong is when we allow them to become our priorities, giving them most of our time, effort and thought: when we are deceived into believing that they are all that matter in life. The result of this is that listening to God and building our relationship with Him gets squeezed out; consequently our spiritual growth is choked, and our spiritual fruit dies.

Secondly, these subtle pressures, which come mainly from within us, though they are undoubtedly influenced by the society in which we live, are not as obvious as the rocky-ground ones, which tend to impact us from the outside. This makes the former the more dangerous of the two.

The rocks spoil the root, whereas the thorns spoil the fruit. Satan doesn't want us to be fruitful for God. So if he can't stop the root, he'll try to choke the fruit.

Fruitful ground (Matthew 13:8, 23)

Here we see what happens when the seed falls on good soil: it produces an excellent crop. This emphasises the fact that it is not the fault of the message that there has been little response so far: the fault lies with the hearers. As soon as that same seed lands on good ground, it is productive and shows results. The difference between this type of ground and the others can be summed up in one word: fruitfulness.

These hearers not only hear the message, but allow it to take root, apply it, and are changed by it. And the result is that they bear much fruit, which is not only a mark of discipleship, but also brings glory to God. Indeed, this is God's desire for each one of us. Jesus said: '"This is to my Father's glory, that you bear much fruit, showing yourselves to be my disciples"' (John 15:8).

There were those, like the disciples, who responded to Jesus' message of the Kingdom and committed themselves whole-heartedly to it. Similarly, this type of ground represents all those who have responded to the message of the Gospel, with the fruit of transformation being evident in their lives. But God wants us to go on from there, and bear fruit for His glory for the rest of our lives, just as the disciples did. The apostle Paul says that we have been saved 'in order that we might bear fruit to God' (Romans 7:4).

In his epistles, Paul identifies three main areas of fruitful-ness. Firstly, there is the fruit of righteousness (Ephesians 5:8-10; Philippians 1:9-11). 'Righteousness' simply means doing what is right in God's sight: living a life that is holy and pleas-ing to God in every respect. Secondly, there is the fruit of good works (Colossians 1:10). Thirdly, there is the fruit of the Spirit: love, joy, peace, patience, kindness, goodness, faithfulness, gentleness, and self-control (Galatians 5:22, 23).

In other words: how we live, what we do for others, and the sort of people we are. God is looking for fruit in our lifestyles and standards; in our willingness to accept our responsibilities towards others and to act accordingly; and in the attitudes and characteristics that we display. In Luke's account this is said to be evidence of 'a noble and good heart', and is a crop that can come to fruition only 'by persevering' (8:15).

The crop yield of 'a hundred, sixty or thirty times what was sown' is interesting. Luke's account only mentions the multiple of a hundred, whereas Matthew and Mark refer to all three. We are not told what these multiples are actually meant to represent. Perhaps they stand for a level of commitment, or maybe it's to do with being profitable servants according to the abilities God has given us, as in the Parable of the Talents (see chapter 10). A third possibility is to do with the number of people who come to Christ as a result of our witnessing.

In conclusion

With the four different types of ground in mind, my prayer is that we will *not* be*:*

− a people who have hearts that are hard, unwilling to accept God's Word (Zechariah 7:12);

− a people who have hearts that are shallow, unable in times of testing to stand firm on God's Word (Ephesians 6:13-18, 2 Thessalonians 2:15);

− a people who have hearts that are distracted, unwilling to give priority to God's Word (Colossians 3:1-2).

Rather, that we will be a people who have hearts that are receptive to God's Word: accepting it, being grounded in it, and giving priority to it, resulting in lives that bring forth fruit to the glory of God.

Questions for group study

ROOT AND FRUIT

Review

1 In all interpretations of this parable, what do the sower, the seed, and the soil represent?

Hard ground
Discuss

2 Why were some who heard Jesus' teachings not prepared to accept, or even try to understand, His message?

3 How is this replicated in some people when they hear the Gospel today?

Apply

4 How should we respond to this?

5 In what way might we ourselves be like the hard ground of the path?

6 What is often the main reason for this?

7 What is the consequence of becoming ground that is hardened to God's Word?

Rocky ground
Discuss

8 How did the commitment of many who responded to Jesus' teachings eventually prove to be shallow?

9 What sort of pressures do many new Christians succumb to today, resulting in their falling away from their faith after an initial burst of enthusiasm?

10 What particular opposition did many of the early Christians have to face?

Apply
11 What can we do to make sure that we withstand the pressures that come our way?
12 What implications does this have for us on a daily basis?

Thorny ground
Discuss
13 When does the choking process usually start?
14 Why does it start?

Apply
15 What four particular areas are identified for us to watch out for?
16 What is the subtlety of the thorny ground?
17 What is Satan seeking to deceive us into believing?
18 What is the result of allowing ourselves to be deceived in any of these ways?

Discuss
19 Which are the more dangerous: rocky ground pressures, or thorny ground pressures?

Fruitful ground

Discuss

20 In what ways are the hearers represented by this ground
    different from the others?

21 How does bearing much fruit bring glory to God?
    (See John 15:8)

22 What kind of people does this ground represent?

Apply

23 The apostle Paul tells us that we have been saved to bear
    fruit (Romans 7:4). What areas of fruitfulness does he
    identify in the following references: Ephesians 5:8-10,
    Philippians 1:9-11; Colossians 1:10; Galatians 5:22, 23?

24 What implications does this have for the way we live our
    lives?

25 In which of these areas do we find the most difficult to
    make progress?

Discuss

26 What possible explanations are there of the phrase
    'a hundred, sixty or thirty times what was sown' ?

For personal prayer and reflection

Do I use the negative response to the Gospel that I may get from some people as a stimulus to prayer?

Do I allow God's Word to take root and bear fruit in my life?

Which of the rocky ground pressures give me the most problems?

What do I need to do to combat this?

Am I putting down deep roots by deepening my knowledge of God's Word, and my personal relationship with Him, on a daily basis?

To which of the thorny ground pressures am I prone to succumb?

In which areas of my life am I bearing fruit for God?

Which areas are in need of some cultivation?

Chapter **3**

THE CRAZY EMPLOYER

The Hiring (1-7)

This parable about the Kingdom begins in a town market place at about six o'clock in the morning. In those days, as in many countries today, there was no welfare system or unemployment benefit; so if you didn't work, you starved. The market place became a sort of Job Centre, where all the unemployed men of the town would gather in the hope of getting a day's work.

A local landowner arrives, looking to hire men to work in his vineyard for the day. There are no Trade Unions, and there is no minimum wage, so he agrees to pay them a denarius for their labour. This is the going rate at the time; in fact, it is the wage received by a Roman soldier. He hires more men at nine, twelve, three and five o'clock, although, interestingly, he does not agree a rate of pay with these four groups of workers: he simply tells them, 'I will pay you whatever is right' (4).

The Paying (8-15)

At six o'clock, the foreman is instructed to pay the labourers, beginning with those who were hired last, which is most unusual. I can just imagine their faces when they are given a denarius each, knowing they have received a full day's wage for just one hour's work. I can also imagine what they must have been thinking: this employer is crazy; what a way to run a business; he won't last long with a pay policy like this; still, why should we grumble! And off they go, scarcely believing their good fortune.

The same happens to the other three groups who also started later: they are all given one denarius apiece. News of this filters back down the line of waiting workers until it reaches the ears of the group who've been there all day. Not unnaturally, they think they're on for a fairly hefty bonus, having worked twelve times as long as the last group to be hired (10). But they are paid exactly the same as everyone else: one denarius each.

They feel they are the victims of an injustice, and you can see their point (12b). But in fact no injustice has actually been done at all (13). They have made the wrong assumptions in thinking they are bound to get a bonus. They have difficulty coping with the landowner's perspective, which is completely different from theirs. What he has done is beyond their comprehension.

The generosity of God

This is a parable about the generosity of God. We cannot earn entry into the Kingdom of Heaven. Our own achievements, merit, even our length of service to God, don't count. There is nothing we can do in our own strength to be accepted into the Kingdom. This would have upset the Pharisees no end.

It is also bad news for all cults and other religions. Every one of them teaches that in some way we can earn our own salvation. And it is an attractive idea to a society and culture that encourages self-sufficiency and personal achievement. However, whatever goal is set in order to achieve salvation, it is bound to be easier for some to achieve than others, which immediately makes it unfair. The only way to make entry into the Kingdom equally fair and open to everyone, irrespective of background, culture, colour, intellect, physique, capabilities, environment, upbringing, and all the other factors that differentiate us, is to offer it as a gift. And that is exactly what God in His generosity and grace has done.

The apostle Paul describes the generosity of God's grace in this way: 'In him we have redemption through his blood, the forgiveness of sins, in accordance with the riches of God's grace that he lavished on us with all wisdom and understanding' (Ephesians 1:7, 8). He also makes it very clear that our salvation is not a reward for the effort we have made when he writes: 'For it is by grace you have been saved . . . not by works, so that no-one can boast' (Ephesians 2:8, 9). The kingdom of this world is about getting what we deserve through our own efforts, whereas the Kingdom of God is about getting what we don't deserve through no effort of our own.

'Too cheap'
I heard of a miner who wanted to believe that God would forgive his sins and welcome him into the Kingdom, but he couldn't believe that God would forgive him if he just turned

to Him and asked Him to. That, he felt, was 'too cheap'. He discussed this with a friend, and the conversation went something like this:

'You were working in the mine today. How did you get out of the pit?'

'The way I usually do; I got into the cage and was pulled to the top.'

'How much did you pay to come out of the pit?'

'I didn't pay anything.'

'Weren't you afraid to trust yourself to that cage? Was it not too cheap?'

'Oh, no! It was cheap for me, but it cost the company a lot of money to sink that shaft.'

At that point, the miner realised that God's grace and mercy towards us is anything but cheap: it cost Jesus His life to make God's generous gift of salvation available to each one of us.

The 'six o'clock worker' syndrome

Even though we may know all this, it is still possible to have the same attitude as the 'six o'clock workers' when we think about people who have come to God on their deathbeds, having previously had no time for Him at all.

I wonder if the disciples recalled this parable as they heard what Jesus had said to the dying thief (Luke 23:43), and how this made them feel. After all, they were the 'workers' whom Jesus had called 'first'. Others had become disciples at various times during His ministry. And now there's this thief: a 'five o'clock worker' if ever there was one. Yet all were receiving the same salvation and the same forgiveness, irrespective of the length of time they had known God. Perhaps, like us sometimes, they wanted to cry out, 'Unfair!'

There is another way of looking at this, though. There are advantages that come with bearing 'the burden of the work and the heat of the day' (12b). One is the joy and privilege of serving God, which brings its own reward. Another is that knowing God means we have a life filled with meaning, purpose and motivation. Workers who come to the vineyard later in life generally wish they had done so earlier. But, at whatever time in our lives we come, we know that we shall receive the same complete forgiveness; such is the grace and generosity of God.

Significant setting

The significance of setting this parable in a vineyard is twofold. Firstly, it beautifully links God's generosity expressed at the vineyard with the Last Supper, where the fruit of the vine represents the blood of Jesus, shed to make it possible for all of us to receive God's gift of salvation and forgiveness, and to be cleansed from all our sin (1 John 1:9). Secondly, the vineyard was a frequently-used symbol among the Jews for God's Kingdom. They were called 'first' to the vineyard; the Gentiles were called later in progressive stages, but with the same privileges and advantages that the Jews had. We have already seen in chapter 1 how the Jews would have reacted to such teaching.

Kingdom paradoxes

This parable closes with a paradox: a statement that seems to contradict itself. Originally, a paradox was a statement contrary to accepted opinion. Jesus frequently challenges accepted opinion. He uses paradoxes to teach the values of the Kingdom of Heaven, as opposed to the values of the kingdoms of the world. Two of these are to be found in Matthew 16:25 and 23:11.

On two other occasions, Jesus uses the particular paradox

found here: '"So the last will be first, and the first will be last"' (20:16). Each time, He is teaching that what is often seen as being of first and particular importance in this world is in complete contrast to what matters in the Kingdom of God. These teachings show us that riches and social status don't count (Matthew 19:16-30, Mark 10:17-31); nor do race, origin and background (Luke 13:29, 30); and, as we have seen already, when it comes to getting into the Kingdom of Heaven, achievement and merit don't count either.

In outer space, directions of up and down, North, South, East and West don't apply: they are relative to the Earth. Similarly, our ways of looking at things are relative to the kingdoms of this world, and they don't apply to the Kingdom of Heaven. As the prophet Isaiah put it: '"For my thoughts are not your thoughts, neither are your ways my ways," declares the Lord. "As the heavens are higher than the earth, so are my ways higher than your ways and my thoughts than your thoughts"' (Isaiah 55:8). No wonder God's generosity is beyond our comprehension!

Questions for group study

THE CRAZY EMPLOYER

Background

1 Why could the landowner be sure of finding men looking for work gathered at the local market place early in the morning?

Review

2 What did he agree to pay the first batch he employed, as opposed to the subsequent groups of workers?

3 When it came to paying them, which group received their wages first?

4 How much were they paid?

Imagine

5 Brainstorm words to describe the reactions of the group of workers who were the first to be paid.

6 What would the group who had worked all day be anticipating by then?

7 Brainstorm words to describe their feelings when they received their wages.

Discuss

8 What do we think about the landowner's actions?

9 Why did the workers have difficulty understanding his pay policy?

Apply

10 What is this parable about, and what does it teach us?

Discuss

11 Why would such teaching have upset the Pharisees?

12 Why is it also bad news for all cults and other religions?

13 What is attractive about the idea that a person can earn his own salvation?

14 What is unfair about such a concept?

15 How has God overcome such unfairness?

16 How does Paul describe God's generosity? (See Ephesians 1:7, 8; 2:8, 9).

17 How is it best to witness to people who think they can earn their own salvation?

Apply

18 In what situation can we be guilty of the same attitude as that shown by the 'six o'clock workers'?

19 Is it fair that everyone receives the same salvation and forgiveness, irrespective of how long they have known God?

20 What are the advantages of bearing 'the burden of the work and the heat of the day' (12b)?

Discuss

21 What is the significance of this parable being set in a vineyard with regard to: the Last Supper; the calling of the Jews, and then the Gentiles?

22 What is a paradox?

Review

23 With what paradox does this parable close?

Discuss

24 What principle is Jesus teaching by means of this particular paradox?

25 Jesus uses this paradox on three occasions, including this one. By this means, what does He teach us might matter in the world, but doesn't count in the Kingdom?
(See also Matthew 19:16-30; Luke 13:29, 30. Note verse 30 in both references).

For personal prayer and reflection

Do I appreciate what it cost God so that His grace could be lavished on me?

How do I show my appreciation?

Is my attitude that of a 'six o'clock worker' when it comes to the matter of death-bed conversions?

Do I rejoice that I have the privilege of knowing and serving God, even though it may be tough going at times?

Does my life reflect the values of the Kingdom of God, or the kingdom of this world?

Chapter **4**

VIOLENCE
AT THE VINEYARD

The Parable of the Tenants

Mark 12:1-12
(also Matthew 21:33-44; Luke 20:9-19)

Introduction

Although this parable is not introduced by the words 'The kingdom of heaven is like', it is appropriate for us to consider it in this section. This is because Jesus, through telling it, shows vividly and poignantly how He – and the message of the Kingdom that He brings – is being rejected by the Jews, and what the consequences will be for both Him and them.

The point in His ministry at which Jesus tells this parable is very significant. He has come to Jerusalem to state openly that He is the Messiah, and is received in triumph by the people, who welcome Him as such. This happens on what we call Palm Sunday, and Jesus will be put to death on the Friday of that week. Jesus spends much of that time at the Temple, which is where He tells this parable. At the time, He is facing a series of questions posed by the Jewish religious leaders in an attempt to give them enough material to use against Him, and to discredit Him in the eyes of the people (Mark 11:27-33; 12:13-27). This is just the right moment for this parable to have maximum impact.

The vineyard

We noted in the last chapter how the vineyard was often used as a symbol for the nation of Israel. In that parable, there was no description of the vineyard as such: but here, Jesus goes into great detail (1a). He deliberately reflects the description of the vineyard given by the prophet Isaiah, where it was clearly symbolising Israel (Isaiah 5:1, 2; see An Introduction to the Parables). He does this so that there can be no doubt at all in the minds of His hearers exactly whom and what He is talking about.

The planting of the vineyard speaks of effort and planning. God had gone to a great deal of trouble and care over the planting, nurturing and establishing of the nation of Israel. It had all started with the calling of Abraham (Genesis 12), and had taken many generations to achieve. And then there are the three Ws: the wall, the winepress, and the watchtower. The wall speaks of God's choice of Israel as His people, to the exclusion of all others. The winepress indicates that He expected the nation to bear fruit for Him. The watchtower is symbolic of His all-seeing eye, which would guard and protect them.

The tenant farmers are the Jews themselves: or perhaps, more accurately, their leaders. This renting of the vineyard (1b) reflected a common practice of the day, with large estates often being rented out to local farmers by absentee landlords. Part of the agreement was that when harvest time came the landlords would receive their share of the fruit.

The servants and the son

However, these tenants don't take kindly to being reminded of their obligations to the owner of the vineyard, and take their feelings out on the servants he sends. Some they beat; others they kill (2-5).

These servants represent the prophets, whom God sent to the Jews down the years with various messages for them, which they rejected, especially when they were about obedience and repentance. The writer of the epistle to the Hebrews gives a vivid description of what happened to them at the hands of the Jews (Hebrews 11:36-38).

Finally, the owner decides that there is only one course of action left open to him: to send his son, 'whom he loved' (6). This reflects the words of the voice from heaven at Jesus' baptism and transfiguration (Mark 1:11; 9:7), and is a clear indication that this particular figure in the parable represents Jesus Himself.

The reaction of the tenants to the arrival of the son is interesting. In Jewish law, a piece of property that was unclaimed by an heir would be declared 'ownerless', and could be claimed by anyone. So the tenants reasoned that if the son of the owner were dead, he wouldn't be able to claim the vineyard, and they could claim it for themselves (7). The son's fate was sealed (8).

They obviously didn't stop to think what the owner might do when he heard the news (9). The Jewish leaders thought that all they had to do was to get rid of Jesus, and then everything could carry on as it was before He appeared on the scene. They would rule the roost once again, and get the people back into line under their control. A few days hence, they would see their ambition being realised, as they came to gloat at the cross (Mark 15:31, 32). But, like the tenants, they had reckoned without the owner.

Action

When he hears what has happened to his beloved son, the owner returns, and deals with the tenants in the most severe way possible (9b). The coming of the son was their last chance: the vineyard is now to be given to other tenants.

The Old Israel, which the Jewish leaders thought they were preserving by killing Jesus, was in fact brought to an end at His death, and the New Israel was established. This is the Christian Church. The Old Israel had been built on the twelve tribes that comprised the nation, and was exclusive to the Jews. Jesus deliberately chose twelve disciples (Mark 3:16-19) to show that He was setting up the New Israel, which was open to everyone.

The Old Israel had not yielded the fruit it should have done, and the consequence of this for the Jews is that: '"the kingdom of God will be taken away from you"' (Matthew 21:43). God's intention had always been that the nation of Israel would be the means of bringing His salvation to the world, but this they had failed to do. Jesus clearly laid the responsibility for this failure at the door of the religious leaders, who had frustrated God's purposes so often down the years and had failed to provide the right leadership for the people.

Therefore, the owner will now give the vineyard 'to others' (Mark 12:9b), representing the Gentiles, 'a people who will produce its fruit' (Matthew 21:43b). This means that all people are now welcome in the vineyard, no matter what their race, colour or background may be. Through the sacrifice of Jesus on the cross, the Kingdom of God is now freely accessible to all who will enter it. In fact, by the end of the second century AD, the Christian church was made up almost entirely of Gentiles.

However, that is not the end of the owner's action. To explain what else he does, Jesus quotes from Psalm 118:22, 23 (Mark 12:10, 11). No longer is He using the symbolism of tenants and a vineyard, but of builders and a stone. Jesus identifies Himself with the stone, which was rejected, just as He was.

But an amazing thing happens to that stone: it becomes the cornerstone of a new building. The word 'capstone' literally means 'head of the corner'. This is such an astonishing occurrence that it is acknowledged by all to be the work of the Lord God Himself (11). And it is by a supernatural act of God that Jesus will be raised from the dead, with the result that He who was rejected will become the cornerstone of the Christian Church. Certainly this is 'marvellous in our eyes' (11b). Matthew and Luke both go on to include Jesus' grim warning that those who oppose the stone are doomed (Matthew 21:44; Luke 20:18).

Reaction

Predictably, the Jewish leaders react strongly to what Jesus has said. They know very well what His parable means, and they also know it's about them (12). They are desperate to arrest Him to show the people that they aren't prepared to stand for this. Added to which, He has publicly exposed their plot to kill Him. However, at this point in the week, the crowd are still on Jesus' side, so they decide to bide their time.

Although Jesus told this parable for a specific purpose related to His ministry, it is still challenging for us to consider how we react when God sends us a message that we don't much like, either personally or as a church. Are we guilty of the same kind of response as that of the tenants?

In the past, being a messenger was a hazardous occupation. If the King didn't like the message he brought from the battle-field, for example, the messenger would be put to death. How often do we in some way blame or find fault with the person who has brought God's Word to us, rather than accept the message and allow God to work it out in our lives or in our church?

Sometimes the sword of God's Word comes to us in all its sharpness, and really hits the spot (Hebrews 4:12). It pierces the armour that we have donned in an attempt to stop it penetrating into our souls. It convicts us, and that's an uncomfortable feeling. But it is these very words that we need to listen to, because God has sent them in love to change our lives, to restore our relationship with Him, to take us on as a church.

The tenants were not prepared to hear God's Word. May the same never be true of us, as we seek to serve God in His vineyard.

Questions for group study

VIOLENCE AT THE VINEYARD

Background

1 At what point in His ministry did Jesus tell this parable?
2 Why is that significant?
3 What did Jesus' description of the vineyard reflect?

Discuss

4 He did this deliberately. Why?
5 What does the planting of the vineyard symbolise?
6 What is the significance of each of these: the wall; the winepress; the watchtower?
7 Who do the tenant farmers represent?

Background

8 In those days, what was the usual agreement between tenant farmers and their absentee landlords?

Review

9 How did the tenants treat the servants who were sent by the owner of the vineyard?

Discuss

10 Who do the servants represent?
11 How does the writer of Hebrews describe what happened to them (11:36-38)?

Review

12 What expectations did the owner have when he sent his son?

13 What treatment did he actually receive?

14 What was the reason for this?

Background

15 On what grounds in Jewish law was this reasoning based?

Discuss

16 What clear indication is there that this particular figure represents Jesus?

17 How did the reasoning of the tenants represent that of the Jewish leaders?

18 What was the outcome of the leaders' deliberations?

Review

19 What had the tenants failed to take into consideration?

20 What was the consequence of their action?

Discuss

21 What consequence for the Old Israel does this represent?

22 In this regard, what is significant about the fact that Jesus chose twelve disciples?

23 What had the Old Israel failed to do, with the result that the Kingdom of God was to be taken away from them?

24 Who are the 'others', to whom the 'vineyard' will now be given?

25 What would be the consequences of this?

26 Why did Jesus go on to use a stone rejected by the builders as a symbol of Himself?

Review

27 What passage of Scripture did He quote from?

28 What happened to that stone?

Discuss

29 Why was this act acknowledged by all to be the work of the Lord God Himself?

30 What supernatural act does this symbolism represent?

Review

31 Why did the Jewish leaders react strongly to what Jesus had said?

32 Why didn't they arrest Him then and there?

Apply

33 How do we react when God sends us a message we don't like?

34 Why does God send us such messages?

35 Why is it important that we as a church are always prepared to listen to God's Word?

For personal prayer and reflection

Am I always prepared to hear what God has to say to me?
Am I willing to allow Him to work out His purposes in
my life?
Do I thank God for loving me so much that He sends His
Word to change me and to restore me?

Chapter **5**

LOST AND FOUND

Introduction

The fifteenth chapter of Luke contains three parables, each of which is about something that was lost: a sheep, which was rescued; a silver coin, that was retrieved; and a son, who was restored. The sheep wandered off and the coin was lost through no deliberate action of its own – unlike the son, as we shall see in chapter 6.

The Pharisees and the sinners

It is important to understand what gave rise to Jesus' telling these three parables. Among the vast crowds who gathered to hear what He had to say were the Pharisees and the teachers of the Law.

The Pharisees were in charge of the synagogues, so

they wielded a great deal of power in the community. There was a synagogue in nearly every town or village. The people used to go there every Sabbath day to hear the Scriptures read and explained by the Pharisees, to worship and to pray. They were not priests, but they were very well-educated people who enjoyed nothing better than debates about the Jewish Law, which they prided themselves on following to the letter. Jesus had some very harsh words to say about them, describing them as 'hypocrites', 'blind guides', a 'brood of vipers' and 'white-washed tombs' (Matthew 23:1-37).

The Pharisees opposed Jesus all the way along the line. This was basically because they were jealous of Him: jealous of His popularity with the people, which they could not achieve; jealous of the miracles He performed, which they could not do; jealous of the fact that He taught with an authority which they could not match. Of all the people in Palestine, they should have been the ones to recognise Jesus as the promised Messiah; but they steadfastly refused to acknowledge Him as such, preferring to maintain their position and their power. Instead of pointing the people to Jesus the Messiah, they made every effort to turn the people against Him.

They were extremely religious, and taught the people that salvation came through obeying every single little detail of the Law. They would have nothing to do with those who broke any of the hundreds of laws involved. These people were called 'sinners', and were regarded as outcasts in proper religious society.

The tax collectors

Also in the crowd were tax collectors (1). This was one of the most reviled occupations, and no self-respecting Jew would do the job. The reason for this was that as a tax collector you worked for the hated Roman conquerors, and were taking money from your fellow Jews to give to the enemy. It's bad enough having to pay taxes to your own government, let alone to the occupying power! It was a well-known fact that all tax collectors were lining their own pockets from the taxes they took, keeping a percentage for themselves before handing the rest over to the Romans.

These people were completely beyond the pale as far as the Pharisees were concerned. Not only did they work for Gentiles, but they showed a blatant disregard for the laws about ritual cleansing after contact with them. And yet it was they and the 'sinners' (1), all of whom were rejects in God's eyes according to the Pharisees, who were flocking to hear Jesus.

Mutter, mutter, mutter

The reaction of the Pharisees we find predictable (2), given that Jesus wasn't only welcoming them as part of the crowd He was teaching, but was also extending the hand of friendship to them by eating with them. Such an action meant that He was accepting them and recognising them as people of value and importance.

This is all just too much for the Pharisees to bear. How can this man possibly claim to be the Messiah, and yet eat with tax collectors and 'sinners'? Surely if He is truly God's Anointed One He would have nothing to do with these lawbreakers, is what they are thinking.

Unlike the Pharisees, Jesus was totally unconcerned about His social reputation. Throughout His ministry He continually went to those who needed Him, irrespective of their back-grounds and social status. The challenge for us as followers of

Jesus is this: Are we also prepared to go to all those who need Christ, or are there some we prefer to keep at a distance?

In response to their mutterings, Jesus told parables to show that their way of thinking was completely misguided.

Searching (4, 8)

In each case, the reaction of the owner is the same. Both the shepherd whose sheep has wandered off and the woman who has lost her silver drachma coin immediately begin a search. If they hadn't taken the initiative in this way, the sheep and the coin would have remained lost, presumably for ever.

The shepherd leaves the other ninety-nine sheep he possesses, and sets off in search of the one which has strayed in order to rescue it. The housewife abandons the rest of her chores, and embarks on a thorough search of the premises in order to retrieve the coin. Both items are of such great value to their owners that they are totally focused on finding them, to the exclusion of everything else.

We might think that the shepherd is rather reckless in leaving the ninety-nine sheep unprotected, but presumably he is confident that they will remain secure while he is on his rescue mission. Besides which, the lost sheep is of great value, so he desperately wants to find it. The woman is probably in a total panic, because the coin she has lost is equivalent to a day's wages, and she can just hear her husband on the subject. It is highly likely that this coin is one of the set of ten which was customarily given to a Palestinian woman as a wedding gift, and thus has great sentimental as well as monetary value. This would make its loss doubly distressing.

Both searches would be difficult. The sheep could have wandered off in any direction; it could be lying somewhere, hidden from view. The coin could be anywhere in the house. The sheep could have got stuck in a place that would be tricky to access. The coin would be almost impossible to see on an earthen floor in a house with no windows, even with the aid of a lamp.

Both seekers could have despaired and called off their search, given that the chances of success were so small. But they didn't. The sheep and the coin were of such great value, and mattered so much to them, that they were determined to continue, despite all the difficulties and problems which they encountered during the search, until they succeeded in finding that which was lost.

Rejoicing (5-6, 9)

And what joy there is in the hearts of the shepherd and the housewife when their search is finally rewarded.

What lovely pictures are portrayed here. The shepherd, with the sheep he has rescued laid across his shoulders, carrying it home in triumph. The sheep, maybe injured, with its fleece torn, bruised, dirty, bleating faintly, draped trustingly round the neck of its beaming saviour. 'Rejoice with me; I have found my lost sheep', he cries in high excitement, summoning his friends and neighbours to come and celebrate with Him.

The woman, maybe dancing round the house in a mixture of euphoria and relief, clutching the silver coin she has retrieved. She, too, gathers her friends and neighbours together to celebrate with her. 'Rejoice with me; I have found my lost coin', she declares jubilantly. The extent of their rejoicing reflects the value and importance to them of what they have found.

The 3 Rs: rescue, retrieval and restoration

Jesus knew that everyone in the crowd, including the Pharisees, along with all those who would hear about these parables or read them for themselves, would be able to empathise and identify with the shepherd and the housewife: to feel the pain over their loss; to understand the desperation of their search; to experience the emotions of their success.

'So now you know how I feel!' is what Jesus is saying. His mission involved the three elements of rescue, retrieval and restoration, motivated and underpinned by His amazing love. The first two of these required Him to take the initiative and begin the search for each one of us, so that we need not be lost for ever.

In the words of the prophet Isaiah, which many in the crowd would have recalled as they heard about the lost sheep, 'We all, like sheep, have gone astray, each of us has turned to his own way ' (Isaiah 53:6a). We have all wandered away from God and are hopelessly lost. But, wherever we may have ended up, whatever state or condition we may be in, whatever we may have done, the Good Shepherd loves us so much that He has come to make it possible for us to be rescued and retrieved (John 10:11). In other words, He has come to save us from our sinfulness, and to bring us back into His presence.

As Jesus would explain at Zacchaeus' house as His crucifixion drew ever nearer: '"The Son of Man [by which He meant Himself] came to seek and to save what was lost"' (Luke 19:10). It was these words and the parable of the Lost Sheep that I had in mind when I wrote a song entitled 'He Loved Me', the words of which are appropriate here:

> He loved me; when I didn't want to know him, he
>   loved me;
> When I didn't want to love him, he loved me;
> When I turned my back upon him and wandered away,

He loved me; he sought me; he found me;
Oh what love!

He loved me; in spite of all my sinfulness, he loved me;
In spite of my unworthiness, he loved me;
Though I turned my back upon him and wandered
    away,
He loved me; he sought me; he found me;
Oh what love!

He loved me; taking all my sin upon himself, he
    loved me;
And now I am forgiven, because he loved me;
Though I turned my back upon him and wandered
    away,
He loved me; he died for me; he saved me;
Oh what love!

The depth of God's love for us is shown in many ways. One is by the lengths Jesus went to, namely, death on a cross, to make it possible for us to be saved from the consequences of our sinfulness. That's how much He wants our relationship with Him to be restored. Another is by the fact that God doesn't wait for us to come to Him: He comes to us, right where we are, in the sinful circumstances in which we find ourselves, and offers us his love and forgiveness. It was the apostle Paul's prayer that we might be able 'to grasp how wide and long and high and deep is the love of Christ, and to know this love that surpasses knowledge'(Ephesians 3:18, 19).

Unlike other religions, where man is desperately searching for God, the Christian faith is underpinned by the glorious truth that God loves us so much that He Himself took the initiative, and came searching for us. And He never gives up seeking us: that's how precious we are to Him.

Repentance: the fourth R (7, 10)

However, this loving act of rescue and retrieval can become restoration only if we repent. Jesus mentions this twice, and develops the concept further in the next parable.

To repent actually means to turn around and walk in the opposite direction: to turn away from walking our own selfish and sinful way, and to walk God's way instead. That is the test of whether our repentance is genuine or not. Having repented and asked God's forgiveness, we know that our relationship with God is fully restored.

Clearly, repentance requires an act of will on our part. Unlike the sheep or the coin, we do have a choice about whether we are 'found' or not. God wants to come right where we are to rescue and retrieve us, but we can refuse. And that is why the rejoicing in heaven is about the sinner's repentance: it is not about the planning of the rescue or the success of the retrieval.

The fact that there is such rejoicing just serves to underline how valuable and precious each one of us is to God. He loves the lost and is concerned for them. The challenge for us is this: Do we have a heart for those who are lost? And if so, what initiatives are we taking to seek them out with the message of the Gospel?

Even you!

When Jesus talked about 'ninety-nine righteous persons who do not need to repent' (7b), He was more than likely being ironic. The fact is, we all need to repent, whether we think we do or not. Jesus was clearly targeting the Pharisees with this remark, because they considered themselves to be righteous in God's sight anyway, because they obeyed the Law, and therefore didn't think they needed to repent. They did not see their need for forgiveness, whereas the outcasts did.

The Pharisees would have found these teachings quite shocking, showing as the parables did God's mercy and love towards a sinner who repents. Imagine, then, what their reaction would have been to the parable they were about to hear next.

Questions for group study

LOST AND FOUND

Background

1 Who were the Pharisees?
2 Why did they oppose Jesus all the way along the line?
3 What is the precise meaning of the word 'sinner'?
4 Why were tax collectors despised by their fellow Jews?
5 Why would the Pharisees have nothing to do with 'sinners' and tax collectors?

Discuss

6 Why did the fact that Jesus was eating with such people so outrage the Pharisees?
7 For what purpose did Jesus tell the three parables to be found in Luke 15?

Apply

8 Like Jesus, are we prepared to go to all those who need Christ, or do we as a church keep our distance from certain groups in society?

Imagine

9 Brainstorm words to describe how the shepherd and the woman might have felt on discovering their loss.

Discuss

10 Why did they begin to search?

11 Why were both searches difficult?

12 Why didn't they give up in despair?

Imagine

13 Brainstorm words to describe their feelings when their search was finally rewarded.

Discuss

14 What parallels are there between the searches described in these two parables, and the mission of Jesus?

Apply

15 How is the depth of God's love for us shown in these parables?

Discuss

16 What fundamental difference between Christianity and other religions do we see here?

Apply

17 What always precedes restoration of our relationship with God?

18 How can we tell whether this is genuine or not?

19 What role does our will play in bringing this about?

20 In this respect, how are we different from the sheep and the coin?

Discuss

21 Why is there rejoicing in heaven over a sinner's repentance, rather than about the planning of the rescue or the success of the retrieval?

22 What does the fact that there is such rejoicing in heaven show?

Apply

23 Do we as a church have a heart for the lost?

24 What initiatives are we taking to seek them out with the message of the Gospel?

For personal prayer and reflection

Do I need to realise afresh that everyone needs Christ, no matter who they may be, and change my attitudes accordingly?

Having been reminded of the depth of God's love for me, how deep is my love for Him?

How is this evident in my life?

What do I need to repent of at the moment?

Do I have the will to change the direction of my life in that respect?

How am I seeking to share the Gospel with the 'lost'?

Chapter **6**

THE REPROBATE'S RETURN

The Parable of the Lost Son

Luke 15:11-32

Introduction

There are three main characters in this story: the younger son, the older son, and the father. From the title given to the parable, it would be understandable to think that the story revolves around the younger son. In fact, the focus of the parable is actually on the father, emphasising as it does his love, mercy, grace and forgiveness. In this father we see the characteristics of our Father God writ large.

'Give me'

In complete contrast to his father, the younger son is characterised by utter and complete selfishness. He just wants to do what he wants to do, irrespective of anyone or anything else. He can't wait to get away from what he sees as the restraints and restrictions of his family home. At last, the day comes when he has the chance to break free. So he goes to his father, and makes his demand. And he's not even polite about it: not a 'please' or 'thank you' in sight (12a). Just the two words that sum him up: 'Give me'.

The son has obviously enjoyed the benefits of a wealthy upbringing. His father employs several men (17), and his share of the inheritance is quite substantial (13). He's probably never done a day's work in his life and, being the younger of the two, he has more than likely been indulged by his father.

Double insult

The son's demand and the father's decision (12) would have sent shock waves through Jesus' audience. For a son to behave like this was unthinkable in Jewish culture. It was an un speakable act of arrogance, representing as it did the grossest possible insult to the father. To demand your inheritance from your living father was tantamount to saying, 'Father, I wish you would drop dead!'

The Jewish Law did actually allow a father to settle his estate while still alive, but only in certain exceptional circumstances. And even then, this was only ever done on the father's initiative: never on the son's. And that's not all. The actual enactment of this would not occur until the father died, since he had the legal right to the land's income as long as he was alive.

So in fact what we have here is a double insult to the father. The younger son has shamed him by his demand, and then gone on to insist that this is enacted at once, thus depriving the father of his rightful income from that land. Yet, in spite of this, the father still decides to grant the son's request.

We are actually told that 'he divided his property between

them' (12b). The older son would have been granted twice as much as his younger brother (Deuteronomy 21:17). Apparently, the older son should have rebuked him for what he had done, and sought to bring about a reconciliation between his brother and his father. He did neither, presumably because he couldn't wait to see the back of him. Unlike his brother, he didn't cash in his land, thus allowing the father to retain the income from it until his death.

Get moving

Having got his hands on the money, the younger brother starts packing (13a). He is certainly well motivated to get moving. He's been dreaming about this day for years, and can't wait to get out of here; but he has also made himself extremely unpopular with the local people by what he has done, and he knows that they are not beyond meting out their own forms of retribution on him. The sooner he's gone, the better for him.

I can just imagine him; combing through every room, every outhouse, every corner of the place, gathering all his possessions together. He has no intention of ever darkening the doors of this place again. Soon he is ready to depart, and sets off. He doesn't even take time to say 'goodbye' to his father or to his brother: they are part of his past, not his future. From this moment on, all communication will be severed. There will be no postcards assuring safe arrival or 'Wishing you were here'! He wants to forget everything to do with home: except the money it has provided, of course. Off with the old, and on with the new!

The son's break with his family is to be so complete that he doesn't just make for the nearest city: he actually leaves the country (13b), thus turning his back on his upbringing, culture, lifestyle, beliefs and even language. For Jesus' Jewish listeners, this was a very significant statement. If what he has done isn't bad enough, he's now defiling himself by going to live and associate with Gentiles.

He wants to make a completely new start, living life his way, using the resources his father has provided in the way he wants to without being told what to do, how to live, and what to believe. He doesn't want any interference from anybody. And the consequences are hardly surprising (13c). He wants to taste everything that has been forbidden fruit, because what this new world has to offer all looks so inviting and so wonderful.

Mirror image

Sad to say, the younger son's attitude to his father mirrors that of many people today, both to God and to life. They take for granted what God has provided for them in the form of the amazing, wonderful planet on which they live. They would rather believe that it all came about by chance than that it was created by a loving God, because that means they are responsible to no one except themselves, and therefore can live as they please.

The rules that God has given us to live by are seen as an unnecessary, restrictive framework, designed to stop our having fun and enjoying ourselves, rather than as loving, supernatural wisdom given to help us to get the best out of life and live it to the full. The prevailing philosophy seems to be that we should have no framework or point of moral reference at all: just make it up as we go along. That way we can enjoy complete freedom, devote ourselves to the pleasures of life without feeling guilty, and everyone will be happy and fulfilled.

However attractive such an idea may seem, sooner or later it will be found wanting, and will often bring with it dire personal consequences, as the younger son is about to find out.

Desperate, destitute, defiled and degraded

After he has 'squandered his wealth in wild living' (13c), which is why he has been described as 'prodigal', a severe famine hits the land (14). The young man finds himself in desperate trouble. He has no money, no food, and apparently no friends any more, now that his wealth is gone. He is alone and destitute in a foreign land, cut off from his family and his people.

The depths to which he has fallen are clearly indicated by what happens next (15). He is reduced to seeking help from a pagan Gentile farmer in the land he has made his home. We see a certain irony in the fact that the only work he can find is on a farm, considering it was a farm he couldn't wait to escape from. He is actually faced with having to work for a living: something he has never had to do before. And, to cap it all, he finds himself feeding pigs.

Pigs were unclean animals, according to the Law of Moses (Leviticus 11:2-8; Deuteronomy 14:8). They were to be used neither for food nor for sacrifices. No self-respecting Jew would have anything to do with them. Simply to touch them was to defile himself. Yet here is this young man not only touching them, but feeding them. That is utter humiliation.

But that's not the end of it. The pigs are so hungry that they are eating carob pods. These pods grew on small shrubs and had very bitter berries. Apparently, they had little if any nutritional value, and were so unpleasant to the taste that not even pigs would normally eat them. Yet he longs to 'fill his stomach with the pods that the pigs were eating' (16). His degradation is complete.

Pig-pen perspectives

What a tragic scene Jesus has portrayed. It's hard not to begin to feel some sympathy for the young man, in spite of all he has done. How long it took him to come to his senses we are not told (17a). But eventually, one day as he's sitting there in the field, watching the pigs grunting around him, he begins to think his situation through.

For the first time in a long while he thinks of home, though initially these thoughts are motivated primarily by his hunger (17b). He decides on a course of action, and begins work on a short speech, which he rehearses to the disinterested porcine audience around him (18, 19).

The structure of his speech is interesting and informative. Firstly, he shows repentance. He knows he has done wrong, not only to his father, but before God. This act of repentance is going to require a considerable degree of humility, but he is prepared to summon up the courage to go through with it. Little does he realise that this is going to take place not in the privacy of the home, but on the road in front of the whole community.

Secondly, he shows realism. He knows that there is a price to be paid for his behaviour. He realises he can't just walk back in as if nothing has happened and pick up his sonship from where he left off. That is gone for ever. He must make the best of things; and the best he can hope for is to be made a hired servant, as humiliating as that will be.

Being in the pig-pen, surrounded by the mess we have made of things, is not a pleasant experience. But so often it does have the effect of concentrating the mind, and giving us a true perspective on our lives. Sometimes it takes the depths of despair to bring us to our senses, and to make us see things as they actually are. As the younger son realised, our greatest need is to restore our relationship with our Father. For that to happen, prompted by the Holy Spirit, we have to make the first move.

On the look-out

So he leaves the pig-pen behind, and sets off for home (20a). I can imagine him, rehearsing his speech out loud from time to time as he makes the long journey. How long it takes we don't know, but it's safe to assume that by the time he gets within sight of the farm he is on the point of collapse, suffering as he is from hunger and malnutrition. What a sight he must have been: dirty, dishevelled, dressed in rags.

Suddenly he is aware of a figure running down the road towards him at a high rate of knots. In those days, for an elderly man to run was considered unseemly and undignified. But the father is not concerned about social conventions at a moment such as this. He does not wait for his son to come to him, as we might have expected: he takes the initiative and goes to his son. His compassion compels him, and propels him down the road. Before the son can say a word, the father enfolds him in his embrace, and kisses him (20b). This is a clear confirmation to both his son and to the local community that forgiveness and reconciliation are the only thoughts in his mind. Rejection and retribution are not on the agenda.

In the last chapter we saw how the shepherd and the woman went seeking that which they had lost. This was because neither the sheep nor the coin could return of its own accord. However, unlike them, the son is quite capable of returning on his own. Like all of us, he has a free will to choose whether to do so or not. The father waits for him to return of his own volition, because only then will his repentance be genuine. So he looks for his coming day after day. God is always on the look-out for the repentant sinner.

Surprised by grace

Someone once described God as being the perfect gentleman, who never forces His way in where He is not wanted. His grace is such that He allows us to reject Him and His love. But as soon as we respond and make a move towards Him, He delights to welcome us, to forgive us, and to enfold us in His love. John Newton, the erstwhile slave trader, captured the wonder of God's gracious response to our repentance in the words of his song 'Amazing Grace'.

To say that the son is surprised by such a display of grace on the part of his father is surely an understatement. This is completely different from how he had envisaged their meeting unfolding while he was preparing his speech back in the pig-pen. What emotions must have surged through him as he felt the warmth of his father's welcoming embrace. Not a word has been spoken, yet so much has been said.

The son's response is to begin his prepared speech (21). I imagine that the delivery of the words has changed considerably, from the controlled, matter-of-fact tone of voice when he was practising them, to one of quivering emotion as he is faced with the overwhelming compassion and forgiveness of his father. The sharp contrast between the way he treated his father and the way his father is now treating him, would be impacting his whole being as he blurts his words out.

Symbols of reassurance

The father's response is interesting (22, 23). He does not embark on a speech of reassurance, telling his son that he is accepted and reinstated. Instead of words he uses symbols that say all this for him, but in a much more powerful and tangible way. They bring a reassurance of forgiveness and reconciliation that is visible. So when the son wakes up the next morning, and begins to wonder whether all this actually happened, he will be able to look at the symbols and know that it really did.

God has also given us symbols to reassure us of His love, mercy, grace and forgiveness. These are the bread and the wine, symbols of His body broken and His blood shed on the cross for our salvation (Mark 14:22-24). They are a powerful reminder in times of doubt or uncertainty that we are loved with an ever-lasting love, and that our repentance will always be met with forgiveness, thus restoring our relationship with our Father God. They also remind us that God loved us so much that He took the initiative so that this could happen. In the words of the apostle Paul: 'But God demonstrates his own love for us in this: While we were still sinners, Christ died for us' (Romans 5:8).

✳ Robe

Let's consider the symbols that the father uses. Firstly, there is the robe. Not just any old garment: it is 'the best robe'. This type of attire was made from costly material not normally used, and was worn only on festive occasions. It is entirely appropri-ate for the celebration party that the father is about to throw, and is a sign to the local community now gathered around them that he has accepted his son back into the family. His filthy clothes, a symbol of his sinfulness, are to be removed, and replaced with a rich garment, a symbol of God's righteousness. Some in the crowd may have connected this description with the writings of the prophet Zechariah, who was shown a very similar picture in connection with sin being taken away (Zechariah 3:3, 4).

This is a powerful symbol of what happens to each one of us when he repents and is made righteous in God's sight through Jesus' death on the cross. As the apostle Paul wrote: 'This righteousness from God comes through faith in Jesus Christ to all who believe. There is no difference, for all have sinned and fall short of the glory of God, and are justified freely by his grace through the redemption that came by Jesus Christ' (Romans 3:22-24).

✳ Ring

Next, the father calls for a ring. This was a signet ring, which symbolised authority: a characteristic of being restored as his son. Once more, he had the power to act in his father's name. And we also have the authority as children of God to act in the name of our Father and His Son Jesus against all the wiles and powers of Satan, as he seeks to oppose the spread of the Kingdom of God.

✳ Sandals

Thirdly, a pair of sandals is to be given to the son. These also speak of sonship, and show that he is a free man, unlike the slaves, who went barefoot. We too have been set free from the slavery of sin. As the apostle Paul put it: 'So you are no longer a slave, but a son; and since you are a son, God has made you also an heir' (Galatians 4:7). What a glorious inheritance we have to look forward to as children of God (Titus 3:7; 1 Peter 1:3, 4).

Restoration celebration

The reason for the festive robe now becomes clear. The fattened calf is to be killed, and a celebration is to be held. Apparently, such a calf would feed about a hundred people, and the whole community is invited to take part in this act of reconciliation.

And the reason for the celebration feast? According to the father, it's all because a relationship has been restored (24). If someone is dead or lost, he ceases to play an active part in our lives. There is no contact, no interaction. This is exactly what had happened between this father and his son. Their relationship had been fractured: now it has been set right.

This is a telling picture of the state of each one of us before we come to God. Our relationship with Him has been fractured by our sin, resulting in no contact and no interaction. As we saw in the last chapter, there is joy in heaven over repentance on earth. That is extended here to include rejoicing over the fact that our relationship with God has been restored.

However, having our relationship with God restored is just the beginning, not the end. Like every successful relationship, it needs to be cultivated daily like a tender plant: otherwise it will soon begin to wilt and eventually die. If there is no contact or interaction between us and God through prayer, reading his Word and listening to Him, then the relationship will just wither away through neglect. It is also possible for it to become fractured once again by our sinfulness, so it is important that we examine our lives frequently to see if we have done anything that is displeasing to God, and to ask His forgiveness.

Strong feelings

Meanwhile, out in the field, the older brother is still at work, apparently oblivious to all that's been going on (25, 26). When he finds out the reason for the celebration, he is very angry and refuses to join in (27, 28a). This would have been perceived by Jesus' audience as yet another direct insult to the father: not as wounding as the one perpetrated by his younger brother, but hurtful nevertheless.

However, instead of standing on his dignity and demanding that his older son submits to his authority by presenting himself at the party immediately, the father takes the initiative once again. He goes out to where his son is, and resorts to pleading with him (28b). These actions would have shocked Jesus' listeners, as would the fact that the older son proceeds to argue vehemently with his father in a public place (29, 30).

He gives vent to his feelings in an emotional torrent of words which reveal resentment, bitterness and unforgiveness. These are in marked contrast to the love, mercy, grace and forgiveness shown by the father. The fact that he refers to his brother as 'this son of yours' is a clear indication of just how angry he is.

The attitude of the older son reflected that of the self-righteous Pharisees. They resented the idea that God would forgive 'sinners' who repented, as represented by the younger son, and accept them into His Kingdom. They were bitter that God did not appear to be favouring them as they thought He should, considering that they devoted themselves to obeying every detail of the Law of Moses which He had given. And they were certainly not prepared to show a loving and forgiving spirit towards those who habitually broke these very laws which they cherished. Reconciliation was not on their agendas.

That can't be right

I do actually sympathise with the older son to a point. He hasn't cashed in his land: he has stayed at home with his father, has been loyal and faithful, worked hard on the farm, and lived an upright life, for which he apparently has received no reward at all. Yet his brother, who has done completely the opposite, is welcomed with open arms and a celebration is organised. From his point of view, a great injustice has been done.

And for many people it is just as hard to accept that living a good and upright life, though commendable, is not going to bring them salvation. The older son, like the Pharisees, felt that *deeds* were required to please God. From their point of view, accepting sinners, who had done nothing to please Him, just couldn't be right. In thinking this, they had failed to understand God's all-forgiving grace and all-embracing love.

Certainly they had obeyed the letter of the Law, but their hearts were far from God. Not only did they need to repent, but also to show a change of attitude. It is this that the father now tries to help his son to see (31, 32), because he loves him just as much as his other son. By focusing on the legal requirements of their religion, the Pharisees had lost sight of the need for a relationship with God. And the result of this was that they continued to see everything in a legalistic rather than a loving way.

Wrong attitudes

The father begins with words of appreciation for his son's loyalty and faithfulness. Then he reminds him of something he has forgotten: he still has his inheritance to come when he, the father, dies. Presumably, there is nothing left for the younger son to inherit. He has had his portion, and has squandered it. And that will be something he'll regret for the rest of his life, along with the knowledge of how he displeased his father and caused him such heartache.

Finally, the father seeks to encourage a Christ-like response from his older son by trying to help him to understand that this is not a matter of what his brother deserves, but is an act of love, mercy, grace and forgiveness. Tantalisingly, Jesus leaves the story right there. We don't know whether the older son was melted by his father's words, or stormed off, still in a rage. Jesus has laid down the challenge to the Pharisees to change their attitude to the outcasts and sinners of society. It is up to them to decide how they will respond.

A number of Jewish Christians in the Early Church were guilty of a similar attitude when it came to accepting Gentiles into the church. The matter became so serious that God spoke to Peter about it in a vision (Acts 10:1-11:18, and especially 10:34, 35).

Jesus is also challenging us not to be resentful or bitter when people whom we consider to be far worse sinners than ourselves come to faith in Him. Rather, we should realise that, although their sins have been forgiven, their worldly experiences often leave their mark, and bring consequences that have to be coped with. And this is our opportunity to support, encourage and counsel them in a sensitive way, thus showing them the compassion of Christ, rather than subjecting them to an attitude similar to that of the Pharisees. It is up to us to decide how we will respond.

Questions for group study

THE REPROBATE'S RETURN

Background

1 Why would Jesus' audience have found the son's demand and the father's decision shocking?

2 In what way was the son's demand in fact a double insult to the father?

3 What role should the older son have played in this scenario?

4 What possible explanation is there for his failure to do so?

Imagine

5 Brainstorm words to describe the feelings of the younger son as he prepared to leave home.

6 Do the same to describe the feelings of the father and the older son at the departure of the younger son.

Discuss

7 How does the attitude of the younger son reflect that of many people in our society towards God and life in general?

8 What is attractive about living life in this way?

9 What are the shortcomings of such a view?

Review

10 What effects did the famine have on the young man?

11 What did he finish up doing?

Discuss

12 How is this indicative of the depths to which he had fallen?

13 What does the content of his 'speech' suggest were his motives for returning home?

Apply

14 What sort of circumstances does it often take for us to get a true perspective on our lives?

Imagine

15 Brainstorm words to describe how the young man might have felt as he:
- got within sight of home;
- saw his father running down the road towards him;
- received his father's welcoming embrace.

Discuss

16 What effect would the father's actions have had on the local community?

Apply

17 What can we learn from this parable about the grace of God towards us?

Imagine

18 Brainstorm words to describe the contrast between the way the son treated his father, and the way his father treated him on his return.

Discuss

19 Why did the father use symbols rather than words with which to welcome his son?

Apply

20 What symbols has God given us to reassure us of His love, mercy, grace and forgiveness?

Background

21 What did the robe, the ring and the sandals each symbolise in those days?

Discuss

22 What does each of them symbolise for us?

Apply

23 Can our community see the righteousness of God in us?

24 Do we as a church use the authority we have in Christ to defeat the power of Satan?

25 How can our lives testify to the fact that we are children of God?

26 The son's relationship with his father became fractured. How can we prevent that happening to our relationship with our heavenly Father?

Discuss

27 What feelings lie beneath the torrent of words expressed to the father by the older son?

28 Does the older son merit any sympathy?

29 How did his attitude reflect that of the Pharisees?

30 What challenge was Jesus laying down to them in the words of the father?

Background

31 How were some Jewish Christians guilty of a similar attitude to that of the Pharisees in the Early Church?

Apply

32 What challenge does this present for us today?

For personal prayer and reflection

What have I learnt from this parable about God's grace towards me?

Do I seek to live righteously in God's sight?

Do I take authority in the name of Jesus over the wiles of Satan in whatever form they appear in my life?

Do I find myself sliding back too easily into sinful ways?

Do I cultivate my relationship with my heavenly Father on a daily basis?

Am I compassionate and helpful towards people who have been far worse sinners than I when they become Christians?

Chapter 7

KEEP ON KNOCKING

Luke 11:5-8

Written on the wall

One of my earliest childhood memories is of waking up one morning in my grandparents' bungalow, and seeing a large picture frame hanging on the wall. It contained not a portrait, nor a landscape, but the adage 'Prayer Changes Things', written in what could only be described as old-fashioned script. Perhaps it would have been more scriptural, and more accurate, if it had read 'Persistent Prayer Changes Things'. Not as snappy, I agree; but more realistic, if my experience is anything to go by.

A friend of a friend of a friend

This parable is one of a pair which clearly teach that we are not only required to pray, but to be persistent in our

PRAYER POINTS

When you pray . . .

God expects us to pray. Jesus emphasised this when He said to His disciples, and therefore to us as His followers, '"When you pray . . ."' (Luke 11:2a). Notice that He didn't use the word 'if'; He used the word 'when'.

God also has certain expectations of us when we pray. Jesus told three parables to make these clear. The first two teach that we are to be persistent in prayer; the third, that we are to have the right attitude when we pray. We will consider each parable in the order in which it is recorded in Luke's gospel.

prayers. In this particular story, Jesus asks His audience to imagine that one of them has a friend who wants to borrow three loaves of bread to feed a friend who has arrived unexpectedly late in the evening (5, 6). In the culture of the Jews, hospitality was an inescapable duty, and to be unable to provide for any guests was a great shame upon the householder and his family. The only way out of this man's lack-of-food problem is to go and rouse another friend, even though it is midnight.

The friend and his family are all fast asleep in bed. Suddenly they are awakened by a loud pounding on the door. Not surprisingly, the friend thus aroused from his slumber is not in the best of humour (7). But the man is not put off, so desperate is he to fulfil his obligations to his guest, and he boldly persists in knocking on the door until he gets the required response (8). As the Good News Bible renders this verse: ' "I tell you that even if he will not get up and give you the bread because you are his friend, yet he will get up and give you everything you need because you are not ashamed to keep on asking." '

In other words, your bold persistence will in the end result in your prayers being answered. The man showed his friend how earnest he was about his request by knocking until the response came. Jesus is encouraging us to keep on praying, because God does hear us and will answer our earnest prayers.

An American called Admiral Peary eventually managed to reach the North Pole through sheer persistence. He devoted over twenty years of his life in seeking to achieve his ambition. The Eskimos said that he was like the sun, because he always came back. His desire was such that he persevered through physical, financial, and natural difficulties. After he had finally made it, he said: 'For twenty-four years, sleeping or awake, to place the stars and stripes on the Pole has been my dream.' God is looking for such persistence in our prayer lives. The apostle Paul summed it up in just two words: 'Pray continually' (1 Thessalonians 5:17).

Our Father

It is interesting that Jesus tells this parable straight after He has taught His disciples what has become known as 'The Lord's Prayer' (2-4). It's as if He is anticipating the observation that when we pray answers do not often come immediately.

There are various reasons for this. We can easily identify what they are if we consider why parents often don't give their children everything they ask for immediately. It's not because they don't love their children that they are denying them their requests: it's precisely because they do love them. They have a wider vision than their children, who often see things only in the short term. They know what is best for their children, and are concerned for their development as a whole. They know the right time and the right way for a request to be granted, and what is appropriate. They want to see how much the child really wants what he has asked for. They also know that sometimes the answer just has to be 'No!' for reasons that the child could never understand, but which are in his best interests.

Our heavenly Father loves us with a divine love that is far greater than that of any parent for his child. Unlike us, His timing is perfect and He sees the end from the beginning. Our part is to be persistent in our prayers, and to have faith and trust in our Father to answer them as and when He deems appropriate. This has the effect of building us up spiritually.

That time of waiting can be very testing, and if we are not careful, we can become a bit like the petulant child, who assumes that the apparent lack of action on the part of the parent indicates a lack of love and care, when nothing could be further from the truth.

NOT HER AGAIN!

The Parable of the Widow and the Judge

Luke 18:1-8

Never give up

Later on in His ministry, by means of this parable, Jesus repeats this teaching about being persistent in prayer. This is an indication of just how important He considered it to be that we grasp this principle about prayer. Indeed, Luke prefaces the parable with the words: 'Then Jesus told his disciples a parable to show them that they should always pray and not give up' (1).

Interestingly, on this occasion, the person to whom the request is directed, the judge, is not in the least bit sympathetic to the supplicant. She is a widow, which makes her particularly helpless and vulnerable since she has no family to support her and to plead her case. All she has going for her is her persistence. And she is determined to use it to her advantage, despite the fact that the odds are stacked against her.

The legal system at the time of Jesus was very different from anything most of us have experienced. If you were in dispute with someone, you had to get a judge to make a ruling about your case so it could be settled. Most of these judges were totally corrupt (2), and expected to be bribed to find in your favour.

The judge keeps putting her off, probably in the expectation of a bribe (4a), but the widow has nothing to bribe him with. All she can hope to do is to wear him down through her persistence. Everywhere he goes, she dogs his footsteps. When he leaves home in the morning, there she is. When he goes for his lunch, there she is. Whenever he leaves the court, there she is, asking him to give her justice. In the end, he gets so fed up with her pestering him all the time that he rules in her favour (4b, 5).

Contrasts

Jesus makes His point by contrasting the unjust judge with God. If such an unsavoury character as this judge can be made to act justly through the persistent appeals of this helpless woman, how much more will God, who loves and cares for us, respond to our petitions as we continually bring them before Him (6-8a). He expects us to pray persistently in believing faith, right up to the point of Christ's return (8b).

There are some other interesting contrasts here. The widow was a stranger to the judge: we are known and loved by God. The judge kept his distance from the widow: God bids us to draw near to Him. She came to an unjust judge: we come to a Judge who is holy and righteous. She had no promise that anything would happen: we have God's promise that it will. She could come to the judge only at certain times: we can come to God at any time. May we take full advantage of that, drawing near to Him in prayer at every opportunity, trusting in His righteousness, and in faith believing that there will be an answer.

ARROGANCE AND PENITENCE

The Parable of the Pharisee and the Tax Collector

Luke 18:9-14

The target

Luke makes it quite clear whom Jesus was targeting when He told this particular parable (9). It was those people who were sure that they could work out their own salvation through obeying all the laws of Moses: as far as they were concerned, that was what made them right in the sight of God. They believed it was all down to their own personal efforts: they made themselves righteous. God had nothing to do with it.

Not only were they self-righteous; they looked down on anyone else whom they considered to be unrighteous. It was those people who were represented by the Pharisee in the parable.

Contrasting prayers

At the Temple in Jerusalem there were certain times scheduled for prayer – connected with the morning and evening sacrifices. People could also go at any time for private prayer. The Pharisee and the tax collector are among the crowd coming to the Temple (10). Let's now consider their prayers, and look at the differences between them (11-13).

✳ Which audience?

The Pharisee's prayer is aimed primarily at the audience: the other people who have come to pray. I can just imagine him looking around in a superior manner as he prays in a very loud voice, so that everyone can hear what he's saying. Although he ostensibly directs his prayer to God, as The Amplified Bible renders it, he 'began to pray thus before and with himself' (11a).

In complete contrast, the audience for the tax collector's prayer is God alone. No loud, superior tones here. No looking around at the other people present to impress them: his gaze is focused on the floor. Indeed, he is so ashamed of himself that he is standing well away from everyone else. Unlike the Pharisee, he does not wish to draw attention to himself.

✳ Statement or plea?

The Pharisee's prayer, if such it can be called, is all about how good he is. It is a speech in praise of himself. He wants everyone to know what a paragon of virtue he is in his personal life, and how meticulous he is in his religious observance. Fasting twice a week, on Mondays and Thursdays, is to do far more than the Law of Moses demanded, and he is also very zealous in tithing absolutely everything that he acquires. While seeming to give God the credit for his achievements, he is in fact doing all this for his own honour and glory, not God's. He is so arrogant that he thinks he has no faults, and therefore stands self-righteous before God. His prayer is a statement, not a plea.

The tax collector's prayer, by contrast, is all about how bad he is. There is no speech from him: just abject confession and penitence. No fine words of self-congratulation: just a cry for mercy that comes from the heart. He is not blinded by arrogance: he is only too well aware of his faults. Unlike the Pharisee, he knows how unrighteous he is, so he humbles himself and bows before God in repentance. His prayer is a plea, not a statement.

✴ Bragging or begging?

The contrast between their motives for praying can be summed up in two words: bragging and begging. The Pharisee has come to brag about his righteousness, whereas the tax collector has come to beg for forgiveness for his unrighteousness.

The Pharisee's arrogance is shown as he tries to make a public spectacle of the tax collector, whom he despises. He points him out to his audience, as he brags that he is not like other men, such as that tax collector over there, whom he holds up as the worst possible example of the type of sinner he is talking about. By contrast, the tax collector's penitence is shown as he begs for mercy. Unlike the Pharisee, he has eyes only for himself.

Contrasting responses

On a previous occasion, Jesus had taught His followers the importance of motive when giving alms, praying and fasting (Matthew 6:1-18). If done for the wrong reasons, they were a complete waste of time in God's eyes. The prayer of the Pharisee fell into this category. He got what he asked for: nothing.

Now comes the big shock for those in the crowd whom Jesus has targeted. By contrast, the tax collector 'went home justified before God' (14a). The word 'justified' simply means '*just as if* I'd never sinned'. His sins are forgiven, and he has been made righteous in God's sight, because he has had the humility to acknowledge his sinfulness and to throw himself on God's mercy. Like the Pharisee, he got what he asked for.

More prayer pointers

Jesus' summary of the main teaching of this parable was that God requires us to be humble before Him in prayer, showing the attitude of the tax collector, not that of the Pharisee (14b).

This parable also contains other teaching points that are helpful to bear in mind when we pray:

- Our prayers should be directed to God, and not at others.
- When praying in public, we need to make sure that we are drawing the attention of the congregation to God, not to ourselves.
- God is not impressed by fine-sounding words, but by what comes from the heart.
- It is important that we always give God the honour and glorify His name, giving Him thanks for anything we may have achieved.
- We should not compare ourselves with others, but focus on our own shortcomings, acknowledge our sinfulness, and repent.

- Our prayers will remain unanswered if they are offered in the wrong spirit or for the wrong reasons.

May an understanding of these points, and those we have learnt from the other parables in this chapter, be evident every time we pray.

Questions for group study

PRAYER POINTS

1) Keep on knocking

Background
1 How was hospitality regarded in Jewish culture?

Review
2 Why did the man have to go and rouse his friend?
3 Why did the friend give the man what he wanted in the end?

Apply
4 What can we learn from this incident about prayer?
5 Why is it difficult at times to be persistent in our praying?
6 How can we overcome such problems?

Discuss
7 Why don't parents give their children everything they ask for immediately?
8 Which of these reasons can be used to explain why our heavenly Father doesn't always answer the prayers of His children at once?

Apply
9 In what ways do we need to show faith and trust in our Father when we pray?

10 Are there any encouraging personal testimonies [from the group] of answered prayer after a long period of waiting?

2) Not her again!

Discuss
11 What is indicated by the fact that Jesus tells another parable about the necessity of being persistent in our prayers?

Background
12 If you were in dispute with someone in those days, what did you have to do?
13 What was the usual way of getting a ruling in your favour?

Discuss
14 Why was the widow particularly helpless and vulnerable in this sort of situation?

Review
15 Why was she successful in the end?
16 How did Jesus make the point that God will respond to our persistent, believing prayers?

Discuss
17 What contrasts can we see between the widow as she came to the judge, and us as we come to God?

Apply
18 What can we learn from this to encourage us as we pray?

3) Arrogance and penitence

Review
19 Who was Jesus targeting in this parable?

Discuss
20 What contrasts can we see in the attitude and posture of the Pharisee and the tax collector as they prayed?

21 What contrasts can we see in the content of their prayers?

22 What contrast was there in their motives for praying?

23 How was the Pharisee's arrogance particularly shown?

24 How can we tell that the tax collector's penitence was genuine?

25 How were both men's prayers answered?

Review
26 How did Jesus summarise the main teaching of this parable?

Apply
27 Why is humility important when we pray?

28 What else can we learn from this parable that is helpful to bear in mind whenever we pray?

For personal prayer and reflection

Am I persistent in my prayers, even when there appears to
be no answer?

What am I going to do to tackle the difficulties I experience
in this area?

Do I trust God to answer my prayers how, as and when He
deems appropriate?

How do I react to such times of waiting?

What have I learnt that encourages me to keep on praying?

Do I appreciate the need to come to prayer with a humble
attitude?

What other aspects of my praying have I been challenged
about?

Chapter **8**

ON THE JERICHO ROAD

Luke 10:25-37

Compare and contrast

Jesus told this parable in answer to a question that He was asked twice during His ministry: 'What must I do to inherit eternal life?' (Luke 10:25; 18:18). These two occasions provide a fascinating contrast. The question might have been the same, but the motives of the questioners were very different. The second time it was asked, it came from a rich young ruler who was sincerely searching for the truth. On this occasion, the 'expert in the law' (25) was motivated purely by the desire to provoke Jesus into a dispute, hoping He would say something that could be used against Him.

Interestingly, Jesus' initial response is the same: He refers them both to the commandments as set out in the

Law. But the technique He uses is quite different. In the case of the rich young ruler, He reminds him of the commandments (18:20). This brings out what the young man's problem actually is, which Jesus then goes on to address (18:21-23).

Compare this with the way He handles the expert in the Law. Knowing that these people enjoy nothing more than the chance to debate in public, Jesus responds to his question with one of His own about the Law (26). This was a technique often employed by rabbis during discussion. Flattered by the opportunity to show off his knowledge to the ignorant crowd, the expert replies by quoting from Deuteronomy 6:5 and Leviticus 19:18. I can imagine him; standing there, beaming with pride as Jesus tells him that what he has said is absolutely right (28a). Unwittingly though, the expert has opened up the opportunity for Jesus to address what his problem and that of his fellow Pharisees actually is: hypocrisy. They know what the Law says well enough, but they don't put it into practice in their lives in the way God requires (28b).

Suddenly, the expert realises that his lifestyle is being called into question publicly. The smug smile on his face vanishes, as he realises that he has been put firmly in his place. He senses that Jesus has put one over on him, so he feels the need to reassert himself in front of the crowd. Instead of accepting what Jesus has said with a good grace and going away with the determination to change, he decides to pursue the matter and continue the debate. I suppose we should be grateful to him, because without his supplementary question, the parable of the Good Samaritan may never have been told.

Bearing in mind Jesus' previous reply (27), he asks Him, 'And who is my neighbour?' (29). Again, Jesus does not answer the expert directly. This time, however, He doesn't respond with a question of His own, but adopts a different approach. He gets the expert to work out the answer to the question for himself by telling a parable which will guide him to an inescapable, if unpalatable, conclusion.

Rough and rocky with a reputation

Jesus deliberately chose the road from Jerusalem to Jericho as the setting for this parable. This was because it had a particular reputation that everyone knew about. Of all the roads in Palestine, this was the one where you were most likely to be mugged. It was 17 miles long, and went from about 2,500 feet above sea level to a depth of approximately 800 feet below sea level. It was rough and twisty with large rocks and boulders at the sides of the road, making it a perfect place for robbers to hide, pounce on their victims, and quickly disappear.

Along this road comes a traveller. Jesus' audience already know what fate will befall him: and sure enough he is attacked, robbed, stripped, beaten and left half dead at the side of the road (30).

The two from the Temple

The next person to come along the road is a priest. Apparently, Jericho was a country dwelling place of the priests when they were not on duty in the Temple, so presumably he is on his way there. He is followed shortly afterwards by a Levite, who is a worker in the Temple. Both of them would be expected to help the traveller, but neither of them does (31, 32).

I can just picture them walking round a corner in the road, and suddenly becoming aware of the dishevelled body lying there covered in blood. The priest remembers what his religious code says about not defiling yourself by having contact with dead bodies, so he makes sure he passes by as far away from the man as possible, even though he's not even sure the traveller is actually dead. His religion has blinkered his vision rather than enlarged it, to the extent that it has become an end in itself rather than a means to an end. He is more concerned with upholding the tenets of his religion than with helping a human being in need. True religion is always outward-looking; always looking out for opportunities to help the needy (James 1:27).

The Levite, not so steeped in Jewish religious law as the priest, and overcome by curiosity, actually goes across to the body to have a closer look, but then also passes him by (32, Good News Bible). Whereas the priest epitomises religion without reality, the Levite exemplifies recognition without response. He at least realises that there is a problem, and crosses the road to get a closer look. He obviously doesn't fancy the challenge it presents because he's soon back on the other side and on his way. Like the expert in the Law, they both lack what the Law commands: love.

The demands of compassion

We would all agree that the action, or rather the inaction, of the priest and Levite is unforgivable, and they stand condemned without excuse for their failure to show the traveller any vestige of compassion. But then I have to ask myself whether I would have acted any differently. Suppose I am the one coming along the road and I see a body lying there. Imagine the thoughts that might cross my mind as I am confronted by this unpleasant situation:

'Not another one! It's disgusting that this sort of thing can still be happening on our roads. When is the local authority going to do something about it?'

'Someone should stop and help that poor man. I would, but I don't want to get my clothes all dirty.'

'I can see he needs help, but I'm far too busy to stop. I'll be late for my appointment in Jericho.'

'If I stop and help and someone comes, he'll think I've done it.'

'I really haven't got the time to help. What with sorting him out, reporting it to the police, giving statements, appearing in court: I really can't be bothered with all that.'

'I'm getting out of here before they come back and attack me!'

These thoughts show how demanding being compassionate really is. It requires us to accept our responsibilities, and not to palm them off on to others; to be prepared to get our hands and even our clothes dirty; to make them top priorities and reorganise our lives accordingly; not to care about being misunderstood; to get fully involved and to accept willingly all the consequences of that involvement; to be prepared to sacrifice in order to minister to others.

Jesus' compassion for us required Him to meet all these demands. He accepted responsibility for our salvation; He became a part of human existence and His holiness was sullied as He became sin for us; dying on the cross was the main purpose of His mission, and His whole life was organised with that in mind; being misunderstood by the religious leaders, by the crowd who turned against Him, and even by His own disciples, did not deflect Him from His mission of love; He fully involved Himself in the plan of salvation, and willingly accepted the consequences of that involvement; He sacrificed Himself on the cross to minister God's love, mercy, grace and forgiveness to each one of us.

Cross over

The priest and Levite didn't just pass by the traveller: they passed him by 'on the other side' (31c, 32c). This is the comfortable place to be: aware of the problem, but just looking on and not getting involved.

And we see this happening so often in everyday life. I read about a young woman who was brutally attacked as she returned to her flat one night. She screamed and yelled during the thirty minutes that she was beaten and abused. Thirty-eight people watched what was happening from the safety of their windows, and didn't even call the police. They were aware of the problem, but just looked on and didn't get involved. She died as the result of their inaction.

It's hard to cross over the road, because that means going where people are in their weakness and need, and that takes courage. When faced with such suffering, we find that our frequent reaction is to run away from it, as the priest and Levite did, rather than to confront it. Our Christian beliefs should stimulate and empower our recognition of social problems in such a way that it results in compassionate action and involvement; or we stand condemned, along with the two from the Temple.

My hero!?

In Jewish thinking, your 'neighbour' was in fact your fellow Jew, so the crowd would have been expecting Jesus to continue the story with an ordinary Jew coming along the road and stopping to help the man. But Jesus is about to shatter their misconception in the most dramatic way. It is not a Jew who comes along the road at all, 'but a Samaritan' (33a), an enemy.

The Jews hated the Samaritans with an intensity and bitterness that ran very deep. There were two main reasons for this, and they both went way back into history. The first reason for the hatred was that the Samaritans were descended from Israelites who had contaminated themselves by intermarrying with Assyrians and other Gentiles after the Assyrian occupation of the northern kingdom of Israel in the 8th century BC. At that time, Palestine was divided into two kingdoms, with the southern one being the kingdom of Judah, from which the word 'Jew' comes. Since these Israelites had defiled themselves in this way, the Jews maintained that they themselves were the only true pure descendants of their father Abraham.

By the time of Jesus, Israel had become two districts: Galilee in the north and Samaria. The kingdom of Judah was now the province of Judea. So the country of Palestine consisted of three regions: Galilee, Samaria and Judea. Most of the descendants of the Israelites who had intermarried with foreigners were now living in Samaria, and were therefore known as Samaritans.

The second reason for the hatred was that, although the Samaritans were Jewish by religion, they had broken away and built themselves a Temple on Mount Gerizim. This was blasphemy to the Jews, because the Scriptures said there was to be only one Temple, and that was to be at Jerusalem. The Samaritans also maintained that Mount Gerizim was where Abraham went to sacrifice Isaac (Genesis 22:2); that it was where Jacob had his dream (Genesis 28:10-17); that it was the place where God chose to place His name (Deuteronomy 12:5); and that it was the mountain on which Moses had commanded an altar to be built, rather than the adjacent Mount Ebal as the Jews believed (Deuteronomy 27:4-6). These disputes were still being hotly contested during the time of Jesus (John 4:19-22).

So, as far as the Jews were concerned, the Samaritans were both physical and spiritual half-breeds. The Samaritans were just as passionately hostile towards the Jews, and this mutual hatred had been festering for centuries. The situation was so bad that if a Jew saw a Samaritan walking down the street towards him, he would cross to the other side: and vice versa. But in Jesus' parable, the Samaritan does not cross over the road as the two Jews had done: he crosses over to where the traveller lies bleeding to death (33b). Jesus is about to make a hated and despised Samaritan the hero of His story. The crowd can scarcely believe their ears.

A demonstration of compassion

Of the three travellers who have come along the road since the mugging, this is the one who would have been quite justified, given the prevailing relationships between the communities, in passing by on the other side. Yet it is he who stops and goes over to where the traveller is lying to help him.

Jesus tells us that he 'took pity on him' (33b). This is not a pity which speaks with words, but rather speaks with actions. It does not say: 'I feel so sorry for you lying there in that state. You look terrible. They've really given you a good kicking, haven't they? It shouldn't be allowed, this sort of behaviour on our roads. You're not safe anywhere these days. Well, I must be going, but I hope somebody will come along soon and help you.' Instead, it is a pity that becomes compassion, and displays all its characteristics (33-35).

Let's consider those in turn, bearing in mind the demands of compassion mentioned earlier. Firstly, the Samaritan accepts his responsibility: he stops to help the traveller. Secondly, he is prepared to get his hands and his clothes dirty: he cleans the man up by washing his wounds with the wine from his flask, and uses the olive oil he has in his bag as an antiseptic before applying the bandages. Thirdly, he makes this man's welfare his top priority: he takes him to the nearest inn, and stays with him for a while, which means reorganising his plans for the day. He even reschedules his future travelling arrangements by promising to return. Fourthly, he doesn't care about being misunderstood: what other passers-by think is up to them; he will not be deflected from the task in hand. Fifthly, he gets fully involved and willingly accepts the consequences: it's hard to think of anything more that the Samaritan could have done. A consequence for him is going to be the hostile reaction of his friends when they hear that he has stopped to help a hated Jew. He may well finish up with no friends: showing compassion can be hard in more ways than one. Finally, he is prepared to sacrifice in order to minister: this action has cost him two things that we value highly, namely, time and money. And yet he has given both joyfully.

What an amazing demonstration of compassion Jesus has laid before us here in the actions of this despised Samaritan! What an example he is to each one of us. Yet nowhere does Jesus call him a 'good' Samaritan. That adjective was added later by Luke as an acknowledgement of the fact that everyone recognises what the Samaritan did to be the right and the good thing. Of the three who came along the road, he was the only one to see the man in distress as someone to be loved. The priest saw him as someone to be avoided, and the Levite saw him as somebody to be stared at. The challenge to us is this: which of them are we most like when we come across someone in need?

'Do likewise'

The crowd is still reeling from the shock of the Samaritan as hero, when Jesus turns back to the expert who asked the question in the first place, and now asks him one of His own: '"Which of these three do you think was a neighbour to the man who fell into the hands of robbers?"' (36). Although the expert had actually asked who his neighbour was, Jesus clearly thinks that the more important question is whether we behave as neighbours should do towards those who are in need.

The expert finds himself backed into a corner with no room for manoeuvre: not an experience he is familiar with. He has no alternative but to acknowledge grudgingly the Samaritan, even though he cannot bring himself actually to say the word, describing him as '"The one who had mercy on him"' (37a).

Jesus' command both to him and to us is: '"Go and do likewise"' (37b). Compassion is required of us. God expects to see evidence of it in our lives. And not just compassion towards people we like, or agree with, or get on with. Acting like a neighbour means showing loving care and concern for anyone who is in need, irrespective of race, colour, religion, social background, nationality, or circumstances. The Samaritan ignored all the barriers that sought to prevent him from showing compassion to the traveller, and he has been given to us by Jesus as an example of how we should act.

During the Second World War, many of the British soldiers who were taken prisoner by the Japanese were set to work on building the Kwai railway in Burma. They experienced nothing but cruelty from their captors, and they lived in the most appalling conditions with little food to sustain them. Just before the war ended in 1945, the prisoners were being moved by train to another camp. On the journey, they were shunted into a siding. Alongside was a train full of Japanese soldiers, who were all badly wounded and in a dreadful state. Their wounds had not been treated, and were full of pus and maggots. Many of the British prisoners shared their rations and water with these enemy soldiers, cleaning and bandaging their wounds.

They could easily have 'passed by', and felt perfectly justified in doing so. But instead, each chose to act like 'a neighbour' to his enemies. There, in that railway siding, hostility was conquered by compassion.

Questions for group study

ON THE JERICHO ROAD

Background
1   What did experts in the Law particularly enjoy?

Review
2   What question did this expert initially ask Jesus?
3   How did Jesus respond?
4   What reply did the expert give?

Discuss
5   What did this give Jesus the opportunity to expose?

Review
6   What supplementary question did the expert ask?

Discuss
7   Why did Jesus respond by telling a parable?

Background
8   Why did Jesus deliberately choose this particular road as the setting for the parable?
9   For what religious reason did the priest behave in this way?

Discuss
10 What does the fact that the Levite went over to look (32, GNB) say about him?

11 How was the inaction of both of them in complete contrast with the teaching to be found in James 1:27?

Imagine
12 Suggest some other possible reasons why the priest and Levite didn't stop to help.

Apply
13 Why is it often hard to 'cross over the road'?
14 What reasons or excuses do we sometimes use for not doing so?

Discuss
15 In what ways is being compassionate very demanding?
16 How did Jesus meet these demands as He showed compassion for each one of us in our sinful state?

Background
17 Why did the Jews hate the Samaritans with such intensity and bitterness?
18 How did the action of the Samaritan in the parable reverse the custom of the day?

Discuss
19 How do the actions of the Samaritan display all the characteristics of compassion?
20 Why would the answer to Jesus' question have stuck in the expert's throat?

Apply

21 What implications does Jesus' statement 'Go and do likewise' have for us?

22 Who is included in the term 'neighbour'? What difficulties does this present?

For personal prayer and reflection

When I have the opportunity to help others who are in distress, how do I respond?

Do I appreciate the fact that God requires me to show compassion to others?

Am I guilty of discrimination when it comes to deciding whom I will and won't help?

What other challenges has this parable presented me with?

In what ways do I need to change?

Chapter **9**

SEVENTY-SEVEN TIMES

Matthew 18:21-35

No limits

The Jewish rabbis taught that it was your duty to forgive brother Jews who had wronged you, but only three times. The disciples had already heard Jesus say that more was required of His followers: '"If he [your brother] sins against you seven times in a day, and seven times comes back to you and says, 'I repent,' forgive him"' (Luke 17:4). The number seven in Jewish thinking was the number of perfection; the perfect response to repentance and genuine remorse is forgiveness.

Peter is obviously struggling to come to terms with this new teaching, so he raises the matter with Jesus (21). 'Do I really have to forgive my brother as many as seven times?' is what he is actually asking. Jesus' reply is worse than he had feared: '"I tell you, not seven times, but seventy-seven times"' (22). Seventy-seven times?! I can imagine the expression of shock horror on Peter's face as the truth of what Jesus is saying dawns on him. Forgiving others has no limits; it never comes to an end.

Some translations render 'seventy-seven times' as 'seventy times seven'. This certainly makes the point about the limitlessness of forgiveness more forcibly, but it misses the significance of Jesus' use of 'seven times' juxtaposed with 'seventy-seven times'. It is a reference back to the words of a man named Lamech, a descendant of Cain: '"If Cain is avenged seven times, then Lamech seventy-seven times"' (Genesis 4:24).

Jesus is saying that the desire for vengeance when we feel we have been wronged is to be replaced by the willingness to show mercy and forgiveness instead. Jesus then goes on to tell this parable to make it quite clear that this is what God expects of all those who belong to 'the kingdom of heaven' (23a).

The debt: cancelled

The story contains four scenes. The first one is where the king is settling accounts with a man who owes him millions of pounds (23-27). He has no chance of paying off his debts, and is therefore to be sold into slavery with his family so that the required amount can be raised. References to this practice can be found in Exodus 21:2; Leviticus 25:39; 2 Kings 4:1; Nehemiah 5:5; Isaiah 50:1. It was still quite common at the time of Jesus. All the man's possessions are to be sold as well.

With the prospect of slavery and destitution staring him in the face, he pleads for mercy. He asks the king to be patient with him, promising to pay off the debt as soon as he can. The king is so moved by the man's appeal that he cancels the debt and lets him go. Compassion and forgiveness, two of the fundamental requirements that God expects to see in the lives of His people, acting in tandem. As The Amplified Bible renders verse 27: 'And his master's heart was moved with compassion, and he released him and forgave him, [cancelling] the debt.'

What a poignant picture this is of our position before God. There is no way we can pay off the debt of our sinfulness. The only way we can be released from this debt is for it to be cancelled by the King Himself. Jesus paid the debt we owe by sacrificing Himself on the cross, so that God's forgiveness could be offered to each one of us. When we respond to this and repent, the debt of our sin is cancelled and we are released from its consequences.

The debt: demanded

The second scene takes place in and around the palace (28-30). No sooner has the man been forgiven his debt than he physically assaults a fellow servant who owes him just a few pounds. What a contrast to the humble, self-abasing servant we saw in the previous scene! Now we see him in his true colours. The fact that he himself has been forgiven has had no impact whatever on his dealings with others or his attitude towards them. 'Pay me back what you owe me!' he snarls, as he pins his unfortunate colleague to the wall, his face only inches from that of his victim.

Interestingly, the words used by the man in reply are virtually identical to those spoken earlier by the servant to the King (26): 'Be patient with me, and I will pay you back.' He even gets down on his knees in just the same way. In complete contrast to the King's reaction, this entreaty has absolutely no effect at all on the ruthless servant, who has his colleague thrown into prison until the debt can be paid.

In those days, the creditor was perfectly within his rights either to sell the debtor into slavery and recoup the money that way, as the King was on the point of doing, or to have him thrown into prison. Thus incarcerated, the debtor would have no option other than to sell any land that he had and pay the debt that way, thereby securing his release. If he failed to do that, his relatives would have to rally round and pay the debt off among them, otherwise the debtor would remain in prison for the rest of his life.

The discussion

The third scene involves the other servants in the palace (31). Having witnessed the unpleasant scenario that has unfolded before their very eyes, they must have discussed the options open to them.

One is to ignore what they have seen, and carry on as if nothing has happened. After all, it is none of their business really. And besides, that servant is a nasty piece of work, who will not be above avenging himself on anyone who 'grasses him up'.

Telling on other people seems to be discouraged in our society, even from the time we are very young. The rhyme 'Tell-tale tit, your tongue will split, and all the little dogs in the town will have a bit' is one of my earliest playground memories. The fear of reprisals is a very real one. This was brought home to me very forcibly on the day I drove past a house on which the word 'GRASS' had been painted in very large capital letters. Intimidation goes on all the time, with the result that many people keep quiet instead of speaking out and giving evidence. We even hear of jurors at trials being threatened if they bring in the 'wrong' verdict.

The other alternative open to the servants is to go and tell the king what they have seen. Their distress at their colleague's behaviour compels them to take action. Courageously, they decide to do what is right, and to take the consequences. This can be a very difficult example for us to follow, but God will strengthen us and enable us to do what is right in His sight.

The denouement

The final scene is where the unmerciful servant gets his come-uppance (32-34). The King spells out the man's offence: having been forgiven his debt, he has failed to show similar mercy to his fellow-man.

The punishment meted out by the King indicates that this latter offence is far worse than the original one of being in debt. The former was to result in slavery, which still permitted a certain amount of freedom. The latter deserves imprisonment, which allows no freedom at all, with the pain of torture included.

A permanent attitude

The reaction of the crowd would have been that this man got no less than he deserved. But the sting is in the tail, as Jesus declares: '"This is how my heavenly Father will treat each of you unless you forgive your brother from your heart"' (35). We have been warned in no uncertain terms as to the serious consequences of not forgiving those who have wronged us. It is interesting to note that there is only one petition in the Lord's Prayer which requires us to fulfil a condition in order for it to be answered, and that is the request for forgiveness: 'Forgive us our sins, for we also forgive everyone who sins against us' (Luke 11:4).

This doesn't mean that God won't forgive us until we forgive others, because that would make our salvation dependent on the works that we do, whereas we know that salvation is the gift of God (Ephesians 2:8, 9). Rather, it speaks of an attitude that we are required to live in and to show daily. Martin Luther King, who faced prejudice, hatred, abuse and hostility every day of his public life, said: 'Forgiveness is not an occasional act, it is a permanent attitude.' A forgiving spirit is a major evidence of true repentance.

Genuine and unconditional

Notice that this forgiveness is to come 'from your heart' (35b). In other words, it must come from the depth of our being, showing that we mean what we are saying with all the intensity of feeling we can muster. Forgiveness involves the whole of our being.

The apostle Paul tells us to 'Forgive as the Lord forgave you' (Colossians 3:13). Our forgiveness is to be like Christ's forgiveness: genuine and unconditional. Not like the man who lay on his deathbed, harassed by fear because he had harboured hatred against another person. He sent for the individual with whom he had had a disagreement years before; he then made overtures of peace. The two of them shook hands in friendship. But as the visitor left the room, the sick man roused himself and said, 'Remember, if I get over this, the old quarrel stands.'

Jesus forgave when He was 'despised and rejected' (Isaiah 53:3), and we are required do the same. This will enable us to gain some insight into the depths of His grace towards us. The story is told of how Louis XII of France treated his enemies after he ascended the throne. Before coming to power, he had been thrown into prison and kept in chains. Later when he did become king, he was urged to seek revenge but he refused. Instead, he prepared a scroll on which he listed all who had perpetrated crimes against him. Behind every man's name he placed a cross in red ink. When the guilty heard about this, they feared for their lives and fled. Then the king explained, 'The cross which I drew beside each name was not a sign of punishment, but a pledge of forgiveness extended for the sake of the crucified Saviour, who upon His cross forgave His enemies and prayed for them.'

When we consider the enormity of our offence against God, and what it cost Him to bring us salvation, the wrongs that others may do to us begin to assume a proper proportion.

A beautiful idea

This is not to say that forgiving others is easy. It's hard to forgive when we've been hurt. As C. S. Lewis said: 'We all agree that forgiveness is a beautiful idea, until we have to practise it.' We often justify our unforgiveness with comments such as 'You don't know what he did!', or 'You didn't hear what she said!', and so on. We replay the incident over and over again on the television screens of our minds as a way of justifying our stance. We stand on our dignity, maintaining that we were in the right and the other person was in the wrong.

In my experience, it is rarely as cut and dried as that. There is usually some degree of fault on both sides. We tend to get things out of proportion, exaggerating what others have done to us and minimising our own sins. And the longer it goes on, the more difficult it becomes to resolve.

The apostle Paul was unequivocal about this matter: 'Get rid of all bitterness. . . . Be kind and compassionate to one another, forgiving each other, just as in Christ God forgave you.'

(Ephesians 4:31, 32). As far as he was concerned, forgiveness was a beautiful idea that must be put into practice. We are to apply it in our lives in the most rigorous way possible. 'Get rid' means being drastic with any feelings of bitterness and resentment we may have. It also implies that we are to take the initiative in putting things right with the person concerned.

Jesus Himself was quite clear in His teaching on this subject, not only in this parable, but also on other occasions. We have already noted the condition attached to forgiveness in the prayer He taught His disciples. He also said: '"when you stand praying, if you hold anything against anyone forgive him"' (Mark 11:25, 26), and talked about being '"reconciled to your brother"' (Matthew 5:24). The implication of Jesus' words is that many of our prayers are not answered because we are harbouring unforgiveness in our hearts. Selwyn Hughes wrote: 'Forgiveness is the biggest issue I have had to deal with in my own life, and also . . . I have found it to be one of the major problems in the lives of God's people.'

An act of the will

Forgiveness is an act of the will, not of the emotions. Feelings don't enter into it. If we were to wait until we felt like forgiving somebody, I doubt we ever would. I can't imagine that Revd Michael Saward felt like forgiving the men who broke into his home, robbing and beating him, and raping his daughter. Nor can I imagine that Gordon Wilson, whose daughter died of wounds received in a bomb blast in Enniskillen, Northern Ireland, felt like forgiving the terrorists who were responsible. Yet both of them did so publicly in the national media.

Forgetting is also an act of the will. Forgiveness is incomplete without it. God, speaking through the prophet Isaiah, said:

'"I, even I, am he who blots out your transgressions, for my own sake, and remembers your sins no more"' (Isaiah 43:25). In the same way, we are required to forget the wrongs that others have done to us.

A friend once asked Clara Barton about a particularly cruel thing that had happened to her some years previously, but she seemed not to recall the incident. 'Don't you remember the wrong that was done to you?' enquired the friend. She answered calmly, 'No, I distinctly remember forgetting that.' It is far better to forgive and forget than to resent and remember. The only person who actually suffers as a result of my unforgiveness is me. The other person doesn't suffer at all. I'm the one who finishes up all bitter and twisted inside.

Forgiving love

Unforgiveness erects barriers: forgiveness breaks down barriers. There is tremendous power in forgiving love.

During the Korean War, a South Korean Christian civilian was arrested by the Communists and ordered to be shot. But when the young Communist leader learned that the prisoner was in charge of an orphanage, caring for small children, he decided to spare him and kill his son instead. So they took his 19-year-old son and shot him right there in front of the Christian man. Later, the fortunes of war changed, and that same young Communist leader was captured by the UN forces, tried, and condemned to death. But before the sentence could be carried out, the Christian whose boy had been killed came and pleaded for the life of the killer. He declared that this Communist was young, that he really did not know what he was doing. The Christian said, 'Give him to me and I will train him.' The UN forces granted the request and the father took the murderer of his boy into his own home and cared for him. And today, that young man, formerly a Communist, is a Christian pastor, serving Christ.

Body and soul

God is so insistent that we forgive because He loves us, and knows that forgiveness is essential for our welfare, our growth, and our spiritual progress. That is why in this parable Jesus warns us in such a strong way about the consequences of unforgiveness, just as we would warn a child we love about something that would be detrimental to him or her.

Forgiveness brings healing to the body. Gordon Wright wrote: 'If my years in the healing ministry have taught me one thing more than another, it is that nothing contributes more to sickness than resentment, and to healing more than to forgive and forget.' A doctor in the famous Mayo clinic in the United States went so far as to say that with the aid of an X-ray he could see a stomach ulcer heal before his very eyes when a patient decided to forgive someone.

Forgiveness brings release to the soul. A moving example of this is to be found in the life of Corrie ten Boom. Years after her concentration camp experiences in Nazi Germany, she met face to face one of the most cruel and heartless German guards that she had ever known. He had humiliated and degraded her and her sister. He had jeered and visually raped them as they stood in the delousing shower. Now he stood before her with hand outstretched and said, 'Will you forgive me?'

She wrote: 'I stood there with coldness clutching at my heart, but I know that the will can function regardless of the temperature of the heart. I prayed, Jesus, help me! Woodenly, mechanically I thrust my hand into the one stretched out to me and I experienced an incredible thing. The current started in my shoulder, raced down into my arms and sprang into our clutched hands. Then this warm reconciliation seemed to flood my whole being, bringing tears to my eyes. '"I forgive you, brother,"' I cried with my whole heart. For a long moment we grasped each other's hands, the former guard, the former prisoner. I have never known the love of God so intensely as I did in that moment!'

As someone once said: 'To forgive is to set a prisoner free, and to discover that the prisoner was you.'

Questions for group study

SEVENTY-SEVEN TIMES

Background
1 How many times were Jews taught that they must forgive their fellow Jews?
2 Jesus had already increased this to how many times (Luke 17:4)?
3 What was significant about this number in Jewish thinking?

Discuss
4 Why did Peter raise this matter with Jesus?
5 What did Jesus' reply indicate?

Background
6 How does what Jesus said in reply refer back to the words of Lamech (Genesis 4:24)?

Discuss
7 What extra dimension does this bring to what Jesus has already taught?

Background
8 What was the common practice in those days for dealing with people who had no chance of paying off their debts?

Review
9 Why did the king in the parable show the man compassion and forgive him his debt?

Apply
10 In what way is this a picture of our position before God?

Review

11 How were the man's true colours revealed?

12 How did the fellow servant's response, when confronted, compare with the response made by the man himself when he had been confronted by the king?

Background

13 What would the servant have to do, now that he had been thrown into prison?

Discuss

14 What options did the servants, who witnessed the unpleasant scene, have?

15 Why is telling on other people regarded unfavourably by many in our society?

Apply

16 Should we follow the example of this group of servants?

17 Why is it sometimes difficult to do the right thing in this regard?

18 Do any of the group have experience of this?

Review

19 What is the man's offence, according to the king?

Discuss

20 What does the punishment meted out to the unmerciful servant indicate?

Apply

21 What does the statement made by Jesus in verse 35 mean for each one of us?

22 Why is it difficult to put this into practice?

23 What helps us to get the wrongs done to us into perspective?

24 Why did Paul tell us to be drastic with any bitterness or unforgiveness in our lives (Ephesians 4:31, 32)?

25 What effect can unforgiveness in our hearts have on our prayers?

Discuss

26 What do forgiving and forgetting have in common?

Apply

27 Why is God so insistent that we forgive one another, and warn us so strongly, as Jesus did in this parable, of the consequences of unforgiveness?

28 What effect does forgiveness have on us personally, and on our relationships with others?

29 Are there any testimonies in the group to the liberation brought about through forgiving?

For personal prayer and reflection

What have I learnt from this parable about forgiveness?
What in particular have I found challenging?
What do I find the most difficult thing about forgiving?
What do I need to do about this?
Is there someone I am unwilling to forgive?
How and why am I justifying this to myself?
Is there any bitterness or resentment in my life at the moment
    towards anyone?
How can I 'get rid' of this?
Have I wronged someone, and need to take the initiative to
    sort the situation out?
How approachable am I when people who have wronged me
    want to put things right?
When thinking about the wrongs done to me, do I ever stop to
    consider the enormity of my sin against God?

Chapter **10**

ABILITY AND ACCOUNTABILITY

Matthew 25:14-30

In His service

The word 'talent' was originally used for a unit of weight (34kg), which later became a unit of coinage. Its use now as a word meaning 'ability' or 'gift' comes directly from this parable. Here, the talents represent the gifts God has given us and also other resources that we have at our disposal with which to serve Him, such as our time.

In this parable Jesus makes it clear that God expects us to use the gifts He has given us in His service. Each of us has an individual responsibility to do so, and will be required to account for how well each gift has been used.

Five, two, one

The parable begins with the master about to embark on a

long journey, which means he will be away for a considerable length of time (14a, 19a). He calls his three servants together, and gives each a certain amount of money. To one he gives five talents, to another two, and to another one (15a).

At first sight it may seem unfair to give them different amounts, until we appreciate the significance of the phrase 'each according to his ability' (15b). The master is very well aware of the capabilities of his servants, and entrusts each with the amount he knows he will be able to handle and cope with. It is because he has their personal interests at heart that he gives them different numbers of talents. It is not some kind of perverse handicapping system that he has introduced to give each a distinct advantage or disadvantage.

Similarly, God loves us and has given all of us talents and gifts according to our capabilities and our capacity to make full use of them. This is so that neither we, nor the servants in the story, can use the excuse that we did not serve God properly because we were overwhelmed by all the gifts He had given us.

In the Parable of the Ten Minas, which has a similar story-line, each of the three servants is given exactly the same amount (Luke 19:11-27). This is to stress the importance of collective responsibility and teamwork in the Kingdom of God, along with individual effort and enthusiasm.

Entrusted

The word 'entrusted' (14b) is also very significant, for three main reasons. Firstly, because it implies that the talents we have, which are gifts from God, actually still belong to Him (25b). This means that we are caretakers or managers of these talents, and are responsible to God for how they are used. Secondly, because it speaks of God's trust and confidence in us that He confers these talents upon us at all, and leaves us to work out how best to use them. Thirdly, because it means that we are important contributors by means of these talents to the furtherance of God's Kingdom. He is relying on us to make an impact for Him on the society in which we live by means of these natural gifts, used in the power of His Spirit and under His direction.

Each one of us has been entrusted with gifts from God. These are evident in the things we do naturally and enjoy doing. As we submit these talents to God and dedicate them to His service, He will bless them and give us opportunities to use them for His glory. Sometimes we make the mistake of thinking that unless it is a talent which is visible in an up-front way, then it is not as important a gift. Nothing could be further from the truth. It is because the work of God's kingdom is so wide-ranging that we have been entrusted with such a diversity of gifts, all of which are equally important.

Initiative and responsibility

So, having entrusted his gifts to the servants, the master goes off and expects them to get on with it (15c). He gives them no specific instructions as to how to use their talents: he leaves them to their own devices. He makes no attempt to communicate with them while he is away, nor does he ask for progress reports from them. They know what is expected of them, entrusted as they are to take the initiative in what they do with the talents. Each of them is expected to accept his own individual responsibility to make something of what he has been given.

God has the same expectations of us. Of course we need to pray earnestly that God will lead and direct us by His Spirit, but at the same time we need to be actively on the look-out for opportunities to serve Him in the work of the Kingdom.

There are some challenging questions for us here. For example: When was the last time I actually took the initiative and asked if I could use my gifts in a particular area of church life? When was the last time I saw a need and used my talent to meet it instead of leaving it to someone else? When was the last time I realised that with the gifts I have I could contribute to a whole new area of ministry which would expand the work of the Kingdom in the place where I am? Do I take seriously the responsibility I have before God for using the talents He has given me?

I am not suggesting that we all go careering off like a lot of mavericks doing our own thing. All activities must come under the authority of our church leadership, otherwise there will be chaos, duplication and inefficiency in the work of the Kingdom. But if my experience is anything to go by, most church leaders would be thrilled to find themselves in the position of having all their congregation rushing up to them wanting to use their talents fully in God's service, and asking for or suggesting opportunities to do so. Indeed, one of the functions of leadership is to develop the ministries and gifts of God's people for the benefit of the whole church (Ephesians 4:12).

Impeccable

Let's look at how the three servants measured up to these twin tasks of initiative and responsibility. If I were to sum up each of them in a word, I would describe the servant with the five talents as 'impeccable', the servant with the two talents as 'impressive', and the servant with the one talent as 'immature'.

The first servant gets to work at once, busily using his five talents to bear fruit for his master (16, 20). He isn't arrogant about the number of talents he has been given compared to the others. His focus is solely on what he has received, and how he can use them to best advantage for the benefit and progress of his master's kingdom. He could have lounged around and basked in the glory of the praise coming from others, who would speak about all the talents he had, and how the master must have marked him out for something special, and what a wonderful person he must be to have been entrusted with all these talents. But he doesn't allow any such comments to deflect him from developing his talents in his master's service with humility of spirit.

There are dangers in being a multi-talented person, particularly one who is frequently upfront. Three of these are temptation, jealousy and conceit. Many times we hear of people who are looked up to in Christian circles yielding to the tremendous temptations which they face, and falling into sin. They can also become prey to the jealousy of others less talented than themselves, with the result that their ministry suffers, and can even be destroyed. On the other hand, they can quite easily fall into the trap of becoming conceited and looking down on others not as talented, when they should rather be going out of their way to encourage them and bring them on. Failure to deal with such arrogance and lack of humility before God, who has given them their gifts in the first place, often results in their ministry becoming ineffective. We need to thank God for the talented people that there are in our churches, upholding them in prayer that they might not fall into any of these dangers, and encouraging them as they seek to make full use of their gifts in God's service.

It would be easy for such a gifted person to sit back and enjoy the plaudits he inevitably receives without maximising his potential for the Kingdom, which he has a responsibility to do. Some people seem to think that the talented person has an easier life than those who are not so gifted. Not a bit of it. He or she has the greatest responsibility of all before God, who expects to see all the talents He has given to that person being used to the full. As Jesus Himself said: '"From everyone who has been given much, much will be demanded; and from the one who has been entrusted with much, much more will be asked."' (Luke 12:48b).

Impressive

Every time I read this parable, the servant who is given two talents is the one who impresses me the most. He doesn't bemoan the fact that he hasn't got five talents like the first one. Nor does he jump to the wrong conclusion that his comparative lack of talents means that the master doesn't love him as much, or think as much of him. He knows that it is a mark of the master's love that he has not overburdened him with responsibility beyond his capacity. So he is content with what he is given, and sets about the task of using his two talents to bear fruit for his master (17, 22).

What an example this servant is to all of us! His love for his master doesn't depend on what the master has given him. He loves him just the same, and is just as keen to serve him as is the servant with the five talents. Jealousy has no place in his heart. He has realised that it's not what we have received that matters: it's how well we use what we have received. It is vitally important that we, too, grasp these principles, and serve God in an equally loving and wholehearted way, no matter how many gifts He has given us. Failure to do so means that the growth and furtherance of God's Kingdom will be hampered, as will our own spiritual growth and development.

When he is called to account, something very significant occurs. Notice that the words which fall from the master's lips are exactly the same as those that have previously been spoken to the servant who brought ten talents (19-23). Although he has only four talents to give to the master compared with the ten given by his fellow servant, he has nevertheless done just as well, doubling what he was entrusted with. The master appreciates the initiatives he has taken, the sense of responsibility he has shown, and the faithfulness of service he has given. Both servants stand equal in the master's sight, and receive exactly the same commendation and reward.

Immature

The third servant provides us with a complete contrast to the second. He does compare himself with the others, and discovers that they have been given more talents than he has (18a). This turns him against the master, and makes him very bitter towards him, as we hear when he is called to account. He is not content with what he has been given, and all he sets about doing is digging a hole in the ground in which to bury his talent (18b).

What an example this servant is to all of us: except this time it's an example of a wrong attitude rather than a right one. The immaturity of his response is plain to see in a number of ways. He reacts in totally the wrong manner to being given fewer talents. His love for his master does depend on what the master has given him compared to others. He does jump to the conclusion that the master doesn't love him as much or think as much of him. This brings about discouragement, disillusionment, and ultimately downright disobedience. I can imagine him muttering to himself: 'Well, if that's all he thinks of me, I don't see why I should bother!' as he storms off, with a spade in his hand and jealousy in his heart. Instead of treasuring the gift that he has been given, he has come to despise it.

Through this servant, Jesus is giving us a clear warning of what can happen to us if we start to compare ourselves with others, or to allow jealousy to enter our hearts and minds. God expects us to use each talent He has given us to bear fruit for Him, not to hide it away so it never sees the light of day, as this servant does (18c). God has lovingly given us the gifts that we have to meet particular needs in His Kingdom that no one else can fulfil. How then can we ever despise the talent that the Master in His infinite wisdom has bestowed upon us for use in His service? To do so is to rob God of a vital contribution to the work of His Kingdom, and at the same time to rob ourselves of the fulfilment that comes through serving the Master.

Impudent and impenitent

When he is called to account, the servant is obviously feeling guilty about what he has done, or rather what he has not done, because he immediately maligns the character of his master in an impudent attempt to blame him for his own inaction (24). He maintains an arrogant attitude throughout, showing neither remorse nor repentance. He seeks to justify his lack of initiative, his irresponsibility of attitude, and his faithlessness of service by saying that he lives in fear and dread of the master: so it's all the master's fault that he hid his talent in the ground and has nothing to show for the trust that was placed in him (25a). And so saying, he dumps the soiled, unused talent down in front of the master (25b).

In reply, the master uses two particular adjectives to describe the servant: *wicked* and *lazy* (26a). *Wicked*, because the servant sought to blame the master, who was altogether good, for his response, which was altogether sinful. *Lazy,* because the servant had made no effort to use his talent in the service of his master. He didn't even bank it to accrue interest, which the master would have expected him to do, had the servant really believed him to be the 'hard man' he portrayed (26b, 27).

If he had made but one more talent, thus returning two talents to his master, the words spoken and the reward received would have been identical to those experienced by his fellow servants. Instead, his only talent is to be taken away from him and given to the servant who has the ten talents (28). This is so that the talent will actually be used and not wasted as it has been up to now. It's a case of 'Use it or lose it' (29).

The punishment meted out to this servant indicates the seriousness of what Jesus is teaching us through this parable. If we do not use these gifts that God has given us, then there will come a time when no further opportunities present themselves, and others will be used to fulfil those tasks, leaving us to experience the darkness of knowing that we failed to use our God-given talent (30), while others experience the fulfilment and joy that come through faithfully serving the Master (21, 23).

Dorcas and David

Dorcas is one of my favourite characters in the Bible (Acts 9:36-42). We know two things about her: she 'was always doing good and helping the poor' (36b); and she was absolutely brilliant with a needle and thread and a pair of scissors. As far as we know, this was her one and only talent: the gift of making clothes. And how well she used it in God's service to minister to so many people around her. She was so highly regarded in the community, that when she died they sent for the apostle

Peter, no less, who came at once. His immediate arrival is a further indication of how much she was valued in the church. The widows of the town all brought the clothes that Dorcas had made for them, and showed them to Peter (39). It seems that many of them were not members of the church (41b), yet Dorcas had touched their hearts and shown them the compassion of Christ by her actions.

What a moving scene that must have been: the body of Dorcas prepared for burial, with all the widows encircling it, weeping, clutching the fruits of her labours. It must have been too much for Peter, who 'sent them all out of the room' so that he could concentrate on his praying (40). As he knelt there, I imagine his mind racing back to that occasion when he, along with James and John, was present in another room when Jesus brought Jairus' daughter back to life (Mark 5:37-42). Jesus spoke to the girl in Aramaic. Is that, I wonder, why Peter addressed Dorcas by the Aramaic form of her name, Tabitha? And, just as Jesus had done, Peter told her to 'get up', to which she also responded immediately. What unconfined joy there must have been as Peter 'called the believers and the widows and presented her to them alive' (Acts 9:41b).

In this spectacular way, God was showing His approval of not only what Dorcas was doing, but also of her attitude. She is a fine example of the ideal one-talent person, and stands in complete contrast to the third servant in this parable. Like him, she could have hidden her talent away, deeming it to be insignificant when compared to the talents of the apostle Peter and all the miracles that God was doing through him. She could have sulked in a corner, being jealous of the talents of others in the church at Joppa. But she didn't. Dorcas reacted in exactly the right way, faithfully serving God by using her one talent for

His glory. She took the initiative in using her gift, and took seriously her responsibility for making the most of it. Dorcas stands as a lovely example of how God will honour and bless the ministry of any person who is willing to use whatever gift he or she has received from God in His service. Interestingly, it was Dorcas, not any of the apostles, who had the amazing experience of being brought back to life.

If Dorcas is an excellent example of a one-talent person, then the shepherd boy David who became king is her equivalent as a five-talent figure. He was a songwriter, poet, outstanding musician, military tactician, inspirational leader, war hero, shrewd politician, good administrator. David was bold in spirit, anointed by God, yet modest and personable: and he was loved by everyone. Everyone, that is, except King Saul, whose only talent appears to have been his size and physical strength. He allowed himself to become jealous of this multi-talented young man, and instead of thanking God for him and helping to develop his talents further, Saul determined to kill him. This fascinating story is told in 1 Samuel chapters 16-31.

Certainly David made his mistakes, but he did nothing to incur the king's fanatical jealousy. Saul stands as a warning of what jealousy can do to a person, while David is a fine example of someone who was determined to use all his talents in the service of God, despite the opposition, the setbacks and his own failings. There were many occasions when David felt depressed and discouraged, but he continued to serve God faithfully in all situations, and God blessed him and honoured him for it.

Wait till you get home!

God rewards those who faithfully serve Him, but not necessarily down here. The story is told of an old missionary couple who had been working in Africa for years and were returning to New York to retire. They had no pension and were in poor health. They were travelling on the same ship as President Teddy Roosevelt, who was returning from a hunting expedition. No one paid the slightest attention to the missionaries: people had eyes only for the President.

The same thing happened when the ship docked in New York. The mayor was there to greet him; the band played; the crowds welcomed the President home. No one noticed the two old missionaries as they slipped off the ship. They managed to find a cheap flat, and hoped to find some work the next day. The husband was finding all this more and more difficult to cope with, and was feeling increasingly bitter that the President should be receiving such recognition and such a marvellous homecoming. He told his wife that he didn't think God was treating them fairly. After all, they had served Him faithfully in Africa for all those years, and nobody seemed to care. Nobody had even met them on their arrival home.

His wife suggested that he should go into the bedroom and tell God all about how he was feeling. This he did, and when he emerged there was a completely different expression on his face. When asked what had happened, he replied that he felt as though the Lord had placed His hand on his shoulder and said, 'But you're not home yet!'

Whether we are a Dorcas, or a David, or somewhere in between, we know that if we are faithful in our service for the Master in the situation where He has placed us, then one day we shall hear those wonderful words of welcome: 'Well done, good and faithful servant!'

Questions for group study

ABILITY AND ACCOUNTABILITY

Discuss
1 What do the talents in this parable represent?

Apply
2 In this regard, what responsibility do we each have as individuals?

3 What will each one of us be required to account for?

Discuss
4 Was the master being unfair by giving his three servants different amounts?

Apply
5 Why has God given us different talents and gifts according to our capacity?

6 What does the Parable of the Ten Minas (Luke 19:11-27) stress the importance of, which also applies to each one of us?

Discuss
7 What is the significance of the word 'entrusted' (14)?

Apply
8 How can we find out what gifts God has entrusted us with?

9 Why do we need to submit them to God and dedicate them to His service?

Discuss

10 How do we know whether a gift is important or not?

11 Why is there such a wide diversity of gifts?

Review

12 What did the master not do that we might have expected him to do?

Apply

13 What implications does this have for us?

14 What role does the leadership have to play with regard to the gifts in the church? (See Ephesians 4:12).

Review

15 What is particularly commendable about the servant given the five talents?

Apply

16 What are the dangers for a person who is multi-talented?

17 Why does such a person have the greatest responsibility of all before God? (See Luke 12:48b).

Review

18 What is particularly commendable about the servant given the two talents?

19 What is very significant about the words of praise spoken to him by the master when he is called to account?

Apply
20 What lessons can we learn from the attitude of this servant?

Review
21 In what ways does the third servant contrast with the second?

22 How is his immaturity shown?

Apply
23 What is Jesus warning us about through the behaviour of this servant?

Discuss
24 Why did the master describe this servant as 'wicked' and 'lazy'?

25 What would have ensured his master's approval?

26 What does the punishment meted out to the third servant indicate?

27 Why might Dorcas (Acts 9:36-42) be described as a fine example of the ideal one-talent person?

28 Why might King David be described as her equivalent at the other end of the giftings scale?

For personal prayer and reflection

How seriously do I take my responsibility to use all the talents
God has given me to their full capacity?

Do I know what these gifts are?

Have I submitted them to God and dedicated them to His
service?

How do I rate as a member of a team, working with others
to further the Kingdom?

When was the last time I took the initiative about using any
of my gifts?

What new area of ministry could open up in or through my
church if I began to use certain of my gifts?

Am I guilty of any wrong attitudes with regard to my gifts?

Am I guilty of any wrong attitudes with regard to other people's
gifts?

What have I learnt from the examples of Dorcas and David?

Chapter **11**

RESPONSE AND RESPONSIBILITY

The Parable of the Sheep and the Goats
Matthew 25:31-46

Designation

In this parable Jesus makes it very clear that God expects us to involve ourselves in the social problems and needs of the world in which we live. The responsibility for this is incumbent upon us, and we shall be called to account for the way we have responded in service and ministry to our fellow-man.

As the setting for this parable, Jesus uses a situation which was a common sight in Palestine in His day: that of herdsmen separating their sheep from their goats (32). This was done because these animals are different in nature and behaviour as well as in appearance. Sheep follow, whereas goats need to be driven. Sheep will stay in a flock, but goats are self-willed and go their own way.

Sheep respond to the distinctive tune whistled by their shepherd, whereas goats do not. Our designation as sheep or goat will depend on how we have responded to the distinctive teaching of the Good Shepherd as set out in this parable.

The sheep are gathered on the right of the King, while the goats are placed on the left (33). This is a further confirmation that the sheep have acted in the right way, whereas the goats have behaved wrongly. In those days, the right hand side was the place of goodness, whereas the left represented evil. In Latin, the word for 'right' is 'dexter', from which we get our word 'dexterity'; the word for 'left' is 'sinister', which in English means 'suggestive of evil'. If a person is equally skilled with both hands, we use the word 'ambidextrous', which literally means 'on both sides right-handed'. This avoids using part of the word 'sinister', which might imply that this was an undesirable skill. In some societies, for example in China, people who were naturally left-handed were considered evil. To avoid this stigma, they were often trained to be right-handed.

The service test

The criterion the King applies in designating the people as sheep or goats is whether or not they have actively involved themselves in the service of the needy (35, 36). Such involvement is evidence of their obedience, and separates them from those who have merely paid lip-service to this teaching. These are the people who have actively sought to feed the hungry, to give drink to the thirsty, to make the stranger feel welcome, to give clothes to those without any, to care for the sick, and to visit those in prison. And there are other needs that we could add to this list.

Today there are many excellent Christian organisations

which reach out to the needy of this world and minister to them in practical ways. The danger of this is that the rest of us sit back and let them get on with it. Surely the least we can do is to support them, financially, through voluntary work and, above all, in prayer. We have a responsibility to be actively involved, and cannot palm this off on to others. God is going to ask us what we have done individually to minister to those around us who are in need. There are plenty of opportunities right where we live.

None of the activities mentioned in this parable requires us to be rich, clever, or even highly skilled, though all may help in certain situations. We are not being asked to do something that we cannot do. It is a ministry that all of us can be involved in, and indeed must be involved in if we are to pass the service test. Our attitude should be like that of a nurse who was tending the sores of a leprosy patient. A hospital visitor saw her doing this, and commented that he wouldn't do that for a million pounds. The nurse replied: 'Neither would I. But I do it for Jesus for nothing.'

However, it would be a mistake to draw the conclusion from this parable that our salvation depends solely on the deeds of service that we perform. The teaching of the Bible is clear that we are saved from the consequences of our sin through faith in Jesus and His death on the cross, where He took the punishment for our sins upon Himself so that we might be forgiven and made fit to enter heaven. Our salvation does not depend on works; but according to this parable God expects to see us doing good works as the *outcome* of our salvation. Not to do so must call into question the genuineness of our repentance and the reality of our salvation. The apostle Paul puts it like this: 'For it is by grace that you have been saved, through faith . . .

not by works, so that no-one can boast. For we are God's
workmanship, created in Christ Jesus to do good works'
(Ephesians 2:8-10).

Seeing Jesus

At this point in the parable, Jesus refers to the sheep as 'the
righteous' (37a). 'The righteous' simply means those who do
what is right. This serves to emphasise that the action they have
taken is exactly what the King is looking for in the lives of
those who say they belong to His Kingdom.

In caring for the needy, the righteous have in fact been ministering to Jesus Himself, although they have been totally
unaware of it (37-40). A nineteenth-century painting shows a
long row of beggars waiting in a soup line. They are all dressed
in rags and look disreputable. But around the head of one of
them, scarcely noticeable, is a halo. One of them is Jesus
Himself. Mother Teresa spoke of seeing Jesus in each person
who was in need, and ministering to him as if he were Jesus
Himself.

Somebody forgets

The rest of the parable is taken up with the King's judgement
on the people on his left (41-46). The severity of the punishment they face is even worse than that awaiting those who do
not use their talents in God's service (Matthew 25:30). Failure
to act when faced with the needs of the world around us incurs
God's fiercest wrath.

God expects action, but so often He is disappointed. As
someone once wrote:

'I was hungry, and you formed a humanities club and
discussed my hunger.

I was imprisoned, and you crept off quietly to your chapel and prayed for my release.

I was naked, and in your mind you debated the morality of my appearance.

I was sick, and you knelt and thanked God for your health.

I was homeless, and you preached to me of the spiritual shelter of the love of God.

I was lonely, and you left me alone to pray for me.

You seem so close to God; but I am still very hungry, and lonely, and cold.'

The story is told of a lad living in a poor part of town who was teased by someone who said: 'If God loves you, why doesn't He take care of you? Why doesn't God tell someone to bring you shoes and a warm coat and better food?' He thought for a moment, then, with tears forming in his eyes, he replied: 'I guess He does tell somebody, but somebody forgets.'

Forgetting is no excuse for inaction, though it is possible to live our lives without giving a thought to the needy, since they are often out of sight. This makes it is easy to forget to remember. But they are never out of God's sight, nor are they ever forgotten by Him. Nor is lack of action justified on the grounds that some people don't deserve to be helped. Someone once said: 'Those who deserve love the least need it the most.' I can never imagine Jesus' telling anyone that he or she did not deserve His compassion. Nor is 'compassion fatigue' an acceptable reason for doing nothing. The apostle Paul wrote: 'Let us not become weary in doing good. . . . as we have opportunity, let us do good to all people' (Galatians 6:9-10). God will continually strengthen us to do that which He requires of us.

The church detached

In spite of the severe warning contained in this parable about the consequences of lack of ministry to the needy in the community, there are still many churches which have no such provision in their programme. And in those that do, it is often only a few people with a social conscience who bother to get involved. The upshot of this is that the community regard the church as an organisation that is detached from their problems and doesn't care about them. This, in turn, leads them to the inevitable conclusion that God isn't interested in them, and is therefore irrelevant to their lives.

This is reinforced by the perception that the church is basically a middle-class institution run purely for the benefit of the people who attend it: a bit like the golf club. Of course, one of the roles of the church is to minister to its membership, but its prime concern should be to reach out to the people who don't attend it with the Gospel. And an important part of communicating the 'good news' is to demonstrate that God does care about the society in which we live by actively engaging with the problems it presents, as this parable teaches so vividly. The command to love God is inextricably linked with the command to love our neighbour (Mark 12:28-34). As someone once said: 'The only way of proving we love God is to love men, and the only way to do that is by doing something for those who need most help.'

The church engaged

John Wesley, who lived in the 18th century, is a fine example of someone who put these principles into practice. The Methodist church, which he founded, was originally a social Gospel movement. They worked among the poor, the uneducated, the prisoners and the outcasts. Wesley organised 'bands', which were home groups with both a spiritual and a social emphasis. This movement took the working class by storm, and hundreds of thousands came to Christ because somebody showed them in practical ways that God cared about them. It has been said that Wesley singlehandedly prevented a French Revolution happening in this country by engaging with the social problems of his day.

Wesley's example stimulated others to do likewise, and the 18th and 19th centuries became the period of the great Christian social reformers: people such as Elizabeth Fry and John Howard (prisons), William Wilberforce (slavery), Robert Raikes (education), Charles Kingsley and Lord Shaftesbury (exploitation of children), Dr Barnardo (homes for destitute children), and William Booth (the Salvation Army). Incidentally, Booth was a minister in the Methodist church in the 19th century, but left in disgust at the way it had become 'respectable' and no longer involved itself in social issues.

True, in many countries of the world today we don't face the same appalling social conditions that existed then: but there are still many problems we can engage with. James wrote in his epistle: 'Suppose a brother or sister is without clothes and daily food. If one of you says to him, "Go, I wish you well; keep warm and well fed," but does nothing about his physical needs, what good is it?' (James 2:15, 16). Wesley took this teaching to heart, and said that you don't preach to a man with an empty stomach. First, you feed him: then he'll listen to you.

The story is told of a man who fell into a pit and couldn't get himself out.

A subjective person came along and said: 'I feel for you, down there.'

An objective person came along and said: 'It's logical that someone would fall down there.'

A Pharisee said: 'Only bad people fall into a pit.'

A mathematician calculated how he fell into the pit.

A news reporter wanted the exclusive story on his pit.

Confucius said: 'If you would have listened to me, you would not be in that pit.'

Buddha said: 'Your pit is only a state of mind.'

A realist said: 'That's some pit.'

A scientist calculated the pressure necessary to get him out of the pit.

A geologist told him to appreciate the rock strata in the pit.

An evolutionist said: 'You are a rejected mutant destined to be removed from the evolutionary cycle.' In other words, he was going to die in the pit, so that he wouldn't produce any 'pit-falling offspring'.

The county inspector asked if he had a permit to dig a pit.

A professor gave him a lecture on: 'The Elementary Principles of the Pit.'

An evasive person came along and avoided the subject of his pit altogether.

A self-pitying person said: 'You haven't seen anything until you've seen my pit!'

An optimist said: 'Things could be worse.'

A pessimist said: 'Things will *get* worse!'

But Jesus, seeing the man, took him by the hand and lifted him out of the pit.

Questions for group study

RESPONSE AND RESPONSIBILITY

Discuss

1 What, according to this parable, is it our responsibility to do?

Background

2 What common sight in Palestine did Jesus use as the setting for this parable?
3 Why was this done?
4 What is the difference in nature and behaviour between sheep and goats?

Apply

5 What does our designation as either a sheep or a goat depend on?

Background

6 What is the significance of the fact that the sheep are put on the right side of the King, and the goats on the left?

Review

7 What criterion did the King apply in designating the people as either sheep or goats?
8 How have the 'sheep' shown their involvement?
9 What particular characteristic have they also shown which separates them from those who have merely paid lip-service to this teaching?

Apply

10 Name some Christian organisations which reach out to the needy of the world and minister to them in practical ways.

11 What danger can there be for us because of their existence?

12 How can we support them in their work?

13 What needs are there in our own local community?

14 What is our church doing to minister to people in such situations?

15 What priority does social involvement have in our church?

Discuss

16 Since our salvation does not depend on doing good works or acts of service, why bother? (See Ephesians 2:8-10; James 2:15, 16).

17 Why did Jesus refer to the sheep as 'the righteous' (37a)?

Review

18 Who are we actually ministering to when we care for the needy?

Discuss

19 What does the severity of the punishment meted out to the goats indicate?

20 Why is is that many people either do not involve themselves in such action, or give up after a while?

21 Why do many communities view the church as detached and uncaring?

22 What conclusion do many people draw from this lack of social involvement?

23 What should be the prime concern of the Church?

24 What does this parable teach is an important part of doing this?

For personal prayer and reflection

Which Christian organisations that minister to the needy do I actively support?

How am I seeking to help those around me who are in need?

What part do I play in any social involvement schemes organised by my church?

What answer would I give to someone who asked why they should bother doing good deeds, since salvation is not dependent on works?

Am I guilty of simply forgetting about the needy because I don't come across them?

How should I deal with 'compassion fatigue'?

Do I need to change any of my attitudes as a result of studying this parable?

Chapter **12**

READY
AND WAITING

Matthew 25:1-13

Introduction

Towards the end of the gospels, there is a series of parables which teach that God expects us to be ready for, watching for, and waiting for the Second Coming of Jesus. In previous chapters, we have looked at the parables of the Talents, and the Sheep and Goats, which tell us how God expects us to live our lives until Jesus returns. That is why Matthew placed them in the chapter which follows his account of what Jesus had to say about the signs of the end times and His imminent return (Matt. 24).

However, the first of the three parables in chapter twenty-five is the parable of the Ten Virgins, where Jesus explains what it means to be ready for His return. The other two parables in this chapter focus on the practical, whereas the first one focuses on the spiritual.

The setting for this parable is a Jewish wedding, an occasion familiar to Jesus' audience. On the wedding day, the bridegroom would go to the bride's house for the ceremony. After that was completed, he would then take his bride back to his own house for the feast, followed by a procession of family and guests. The feast itself could last over a week, and the neighbours were usually invited to join in the celebrations.

The ten virgins, or young women, in the story are wanting to take part in this outdoor procession. The lamps they bring (1) would not have been small ones made of clay, because these were designed for indoor use. They would have been torches, which were made up of long poles with rags saturated with olive oil at the top; rags which were then set alight. To keep them burning, the oil needed to be replenished quite frequently. Whether or not the virgins were actually bridesmaids is open to debate. The important fact is that they were waiting for the bridegroom to come.

Five foolish, five wise

Jesus then tells us that 'five of them were foolish and five were wise', and goes on to explain why (2-4). The wise five have taken a supply of oil with them, whereas the foolish five have not. The wise five have given some serious thought to the situation. They have made sure that they are properly prepared; so whenever the bridegroom decides to come, they will be ready. On the other hand, the foolish five have not really given any thought to the situation at all. They have treated the whole matter far too flippantly and casually. The tragedy of the foolish five is that they think they are prepared for the arrival of the bridegroom, but in fact they are not.

The bridegroom doesn't come as soon as they expect, and they all fall asleep (5). Suddenly they are awakened by the shouted announcement of his imminent arrival. I can imagine them desperately trying to wake up, rubbing their eyes, gradually coming to terms with what's happened, and then frantically checking the condition of their torches (7). (Trimming involved cutting off the charred ends of the rags and adding more oil). It is then that the foolish five make their heart-stopping discovery: their torches are going out! Seeing the wise five with their backup supply, they try to sponge off them, but quite reasonably the wise five refuse to help them out (8, 9). (Exactly where the foolish five think they are going to get oil at that time of night I'm not sure, but they are desperately hoping they can find some to buy somewhere. It is too late to put matters right. They are to be given no second chance).

The shut door

While they are away on their fruitless quest for oil, the bridegroom arrives, and the wise five go with him into the wedding feast (10). It is at this point that Jesus uses a very significant clause: 'And the door was shut' (10c). This has echoes in both the first and last books of the Bible. In Revelation we read: 'What he opens no-one can shut, and what he shuts no-one can open' (3:7b). In Genesis we find the story of Noah, who along with his family went into the ark to escape the judgement which God was about to bring upon sinful mankind. Noah having entered the ark, 'the Lord shut him in' (7:16b). As the rains began to fall, and the people realised that they were under God's judgement, they would have pounded on the door of that ark of salvation which God had provided, and they had constantly ridiculed. But it was too late to put matters right. They were to be given no second chance. God Himself had shut the door that had once stood open to them. As Noah listened to the desperate cries of his compatriots outside the ark, he must have been tempted to open the door to let them in. But he couldn't, because the Lord had shut him in.

And here again, God Himself has shut the door on those who have not prepared themselves properly for His coming judgement. The foolish five return, to find that their time has run out. What a tragic sight as they pound on the door, and beg to be let in: but to no avail. It's too late. All that is left to them is to hear the bridegroom's chilling words: 'I tell you the truth, I don't know you' (12). They are shut out of his presence for ever. What a contrast there must have been between the rejoicing on the inside, and the despair on the outside. And Jesus concludes by warning us all to be ready for His coming, lest we be caught unprepared (13).

Well oiled

The foolish five found themselves outside God's eternal Kingdom for two reasons. The first of these is because they weren't properly prepared for His coming. This doesn't just simply mean that to avoid God's judgement we need to respond to His offer of salvation while the door of His mercy stands open. Jesus is saying that we also need to look at the condition of our own spiritual 'lamps'. We are called to be lights in this world (Matthew 5:16). God expects to find our lights shining at full strength and to maximum effect when He returns.

The only way lamps can do this is if they have a constant supply of 'oil'. In the Bible, oil is often used as a symbol for the power of the Holy Spirit: for example, in 1 Samuel 16:13; Psalm 89:20; Mark 6:13; James 5:14. We need to be constantly filled with the Spirit of God (Ephesians 5:18b) if we are to burn brightly and consistently for God in this dark world. May our daily prayer be that of the songwriter, who probably had this parable in mind when writing these words: 'Give me oil in my lamp, keep me burning; give me oil in my lamp, I pray.' Our supply must come directly from God Himself: it can't be borrowed from other people, as the foolish five thought (8). Each one of us is responsible for his own spiritual condition.

Well known

The second reason is because their relationship with the bridegroom was lacking. Verse 12 of this parable is a chilling reminder to His followers of something Jesus had already taught them (Matthew 7:21-23). As far as God is concerned, our day-to-day relationship with Him, and living our lives according to His will, is far more important than all the powerful deeds that we may accomplish in His name. It is even possible to achieve great things for God, and yet find ourselves outside the door because our relationship with Him is lacking. In this dramatic way, Jesus is emphasising how important it is that we have a close, personal relationship with God.

Walking, talking and listening are three crucial factors in getting to know someone and developing a personal relationship with him. 'Walking' represents spending time together and enjoying each other's company. Just as we long to be with someone we love, so we need to spend time in God's presence, giving worship to Him and receiving ministry from Him.

'Talking' stands for communication. We look forward to talking with our loved one face to face, or if that's not possible we use the telephone, or even write letters expressing how we feel. In the same way we need to communicate with God through prayer, bringing both our thanks and our requests to Him, as well as telling Him exactly how we are feeling.

'Listening' is all about hearing what the loved one is saying: sensing his heartbeat. It's so important to listen to what God is saying to us through hearing His Word as it is preached, through reading the Bible for ourselves, and through prophetic words given under the inspiration of the Holy Spirit. In these ways we sense the heartbeat of the One who loved us and gave Himself for us (Galatians 2:20c). God Himself knew the importance of these three factors, which is why He came to the garden every evening to walk with, to talk with, and to listen to Adam and Eve (Genesis 3:8).

Jesus could return today. If He did, would He find my lamp burning brightly? Would He know who I am? Would He find me spiritually prepared for His coming?

Parables about being watchful
Luke 12:35-48

Jesus left us in no doubt that His return is a certainty. He said: '"I am going . . . to prepare a place for you. And if I go and prepare a place for you, I will come back and take you to be with me that you also may be where I am"' (John 14:2, 3). These short parables all emphasise the need for us to be alert to the fact that Jesus could return at any moment, and to be constantly expectant of His coming.

Serving and burning
The Parable of the Servants Watching (35-38) begins with how Jesus expects to find us on His return: serving Him faithfully,

with our lamps burning brightly. If their lamps had not been burning, the servants would not have been able to serve their master properly. Similarly, if we are not on fire for God, because the oil of the Holy Spirit is not constantly flowing through us, then we shall be unable to serve the Master according to His will. Our spiritual condition is so important, as we saw in the parable of the Ten Virgins.

Like that parable, this one is also set against the background of a wedding. On this occasion, however, the servants are waiting for the return of their master from a wedding banquet. When the master arrives, he is so thrilled by what he finds that he rewards his servants in a most unexpected way. In a picture that will become an actual experience for the disciples at the Last Supper (John 13:1-9), the master reverses the roles, and serves the servants (37b). Perhaps the twelve disciples recalled this parable as Jesus commanded them to serve one another (John 13:14, 15), and said those amazing words about Himself: '"But I am among you as one who serves"' (Luke 22:27c). Our reward will be in knowing that we have served the One who came to serve us. Whenever He comes (38), may He find us serving faithfully and burning brightly.

Appropriate action

The fact is that we do not know when Jesus will actually return. On one occasion Jesus said: '"No-one knows about that day or hour, not even the angels in heaven, nor the Son, but only the Father"' (Mark 13:32). He followed these words with a short parable, urging us to go about our God-given tasks, but at the same time to be watching for His return (Mark 13:33-37). He will come as a thief in the night (Luke 12:39, 40). If the householder who was burgled had known the time when the thief would be coming, he would have been ready for him.

We have tried to show such foresight by having our houses alarmed. We hope that the system will never be triggered, but we have seen the need to be prepared, and have taken the appropriate action. How much more important it is for us to prepare ourselves for the coming of Jesus, which we know will definitely happen, by taking the appropriate action. That means living our lives in the expectation that Jesus will return today, and making sure that we are ready for His coming in the ways we have already thought about.

Double duty

The Parable of the Manager (42-48) presents us with a picture of how we should spend our time while we are waiting for Jesus' return (42-44), and how we should not (45). God expects us to fulfil the duties that He has given us to care for others, both in the church and in the community. Failure to do so will have the most drastic consequences (46-48a), according to the culpability of the individual; a topic which is developed by the apostle Paul in Romans 2:12-16.

It is also possible to see teaching about the responsibilities of leadership in this parable. If the manager cares properly for those in his charge, he will be rewarded (44); if he does not, then he will be severely dealt with (46b). He is also expected to conduct himself in a proper manner as befits his calling. These two principles of duty of care and duty of conduct had already been clearly set out in the Old Testament (Isaiah 56:10-12; Jeremiah 23:2; Ezekiel 34:1-10). Jesus got very angry with the Jewish religious leaders of His day because they were completely failing to fulfil both these duties (Matthew 23:1-36). And they are still required of all those who aspire to positions of leadership in the church today, along with other qualifications besides (1 Timothy 3:1-7; Titus 1:6-9). As we noted in chapter 10, much is demanded and asked of those to whom much has been given and entrusted (48b), and this certainly applies to many of our leaders. All of which should inspire us to pray continually for them, that they may know God's strength, power and wisdom in carrying out their duties.

Conclusion

Indeed, may each one of us experience God's empowering in our lives daily, as we seek to apply both the encouraging and the uncomfortable lessons that we have learnt from all these pointed and personal parables – until Jesus comes again.

Questions for group study

READY AND WAITING

The Parable of the Ten Virgins

Background
1 What was the usual procedure at a Jewish wedding?
2 What would the virgins have been waiting to take part in?
3 What sort of lamp would they have brought with them?

Review
4 In what respect are five of them 'wise' and the other five 'foolish'?

Discuss
5 What is the real tragedy of the foolish five?

Review
6 Why did they all fall asleep?

Background
7 What did the trimming process involve?

Review
8 On what grounds did the 'wise' refuse to help the 'foolish'?

Discuss
9 What is the significance of the phrase 'And the door was shut' (Matthew 25:10c)?

10 How is what happened in this parable similar to what took place when Noah was in the ark? (See Genesis 7:16b).

Imagine
11 Brainstorm words to describe how the foolish virgins would have felt when they returned to find the door shut.

Review
12 What did the bridegroom say to them through the shut door?

Apply
13 What warning is Jesus giving us in verse 13 ?

14 In what sense do we each have a lamp?

15 How can we make sure it burns brightly and consistently?

Background
16 For what is oil often used as a symbol in the Bible?

Apply
17 What lesson can we learn from the fact that the 'foolish' weren't able to borrow oil from the 'wise'?

Discuss
18 Apart from not being properly prepared for the bridegroom's coming, why else were the 'foolish' excluded?

Apply
19 What does this teach us about our relationship with God? In what ways can this be strengthened and deepened?

Parables about being watchful

Review

20 How did the master reward his servants?

Discuss

21 Why did he reward them in this unexpected way?

Apply

22 What can we learn from this?

23 Given that no one knows when Jesus will actually return, how should we live our lives while we are waiting?

For personal prayer and reflection

In what condition is my spiritual 'lamp'?

Am I asking God daily to fill me with the oil of His Spirit so I can burn brightly and to maximum effect?

If Jesus returned today, would He know who I am?

How much time do I spend worshipping God; praying to God; listening to what God is saying to me?

Am I prepared for His coming?

Will Jesus be thrilled at my readiness and my faithfulness when He returns?

Am I fulfilling the duties God has given me to do while awaiting Jesus' return?

Notes

Notes

Notes